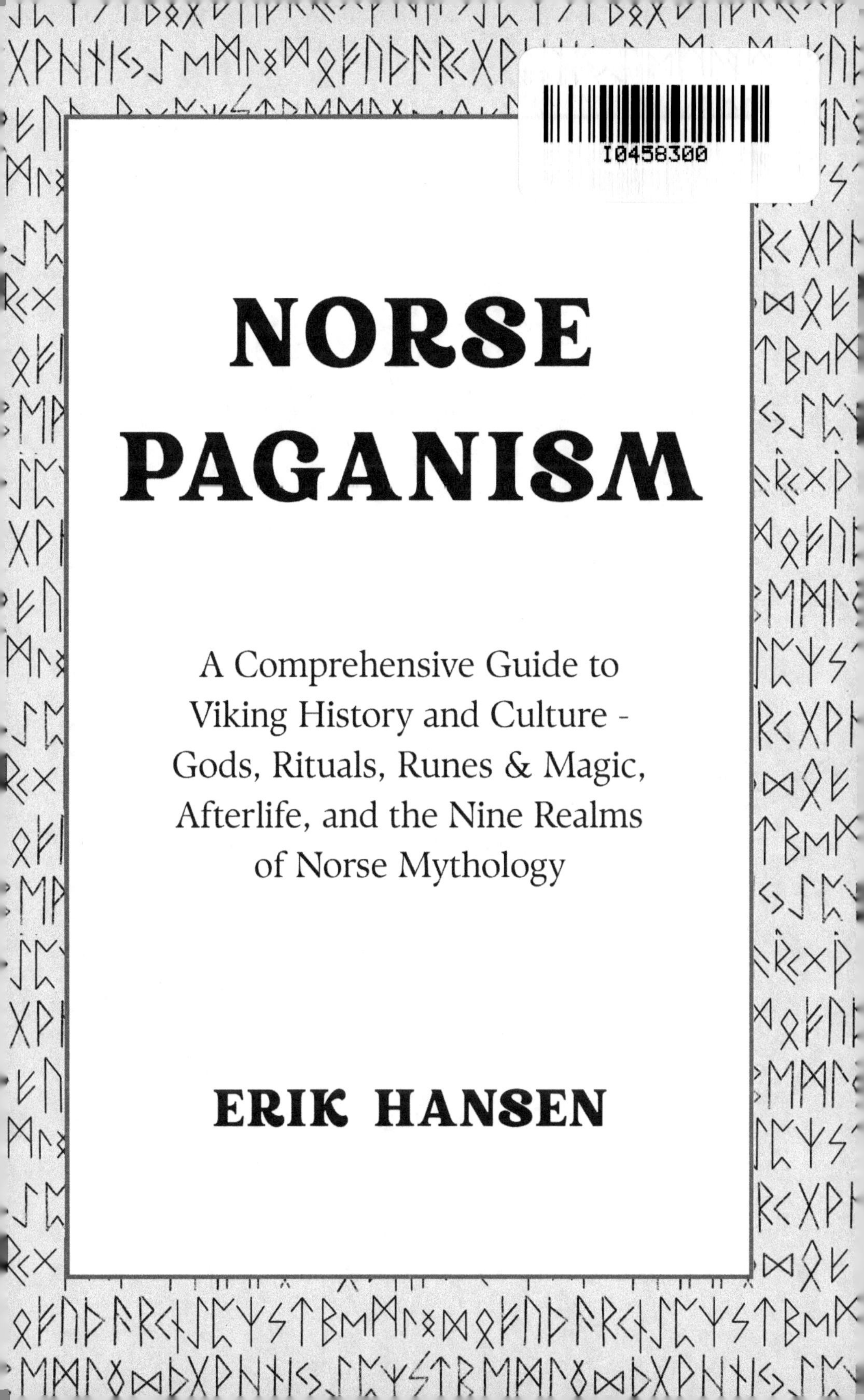

NORSE PAGANISM

A Comprehensive Guide to Viking History and Culture - Gods, Rituals, Runes & Magic, Afterlife, and the Nine Realms of Norse Mythology

ERIK HANSEN

For permission requests, please contact:
Novus Liber Publishing
Email: info@yourbookshelf.top

First edition February 2025
Revised edition April 2026

Paperback ISBN 978-1-961963-55-9

To my beloved son

Be strong when you are weak, be brave when you are scared, be humble when your are victorious.

Contents

Introduction

SKOL! Welcome to one of history's most captivating religious traditions — a world of many gods, fearless warriors, sorcerous women, and a cosmos that was always, inevitably, hurtling toward its own destruction.

Norse Paganism is a strange and thrilling thing to study. It is a religion that produced some of the greatest explorers the world has ever seen, and yet left us with frustratingly little written evidence of what its followers actually believed. It gave us Odin, a god who willingly hung himself from a tree for nine days to gain wisdom — and Thor, whose answer to most problems was a hammer. It described an afterlife where dead warriors feast, spar, and get killed again every single day, only to be resurrected in time for dinner. And it prophesied its own apocalypse in vivid, almost cheerful detail.

This book traces Norse Paganism across thousands of years, beginning long before the Viking Age — back to 10,000 B.C.E., when the first people arrived in Scandinavia and left behind almost nothing except the quiet suggestion that they were already reaching toward the divine. We will move through the Bronze Age and the Iron Age, tracking what the archaeological record can tell us about the beliefs taking shape beneath the surface. We will spend time in the Viking Age itself, looking past the horned helmets and the Hollywood drama at the real texture of those lives: the farms, the raids, the ships, the gods. And we will follow the story all the way to the present day, where Norse Paganism is experiencing a quiet but genuine revival.

One thing that sets this religion apart immediately is its relationship with its gods. Ask a Christian, a Muslim, or a Jew how many gods they worship and the answer is one — the same one, singular and absolute. Ask a Norse Pagan and the question barely makes sense. There are the Aesir and the Vanir, two distinct tribes of deities who once went to war with each other. There is Odin, the all-father, who sacrificed an eye for knowledge and would sacrifice far more before it was over. There is Thor, the thunderer, who is both protector of humanity and enthusiastic slayer of giants. There is Loki, who is — complicated. And there are dozens more, each with their own stories, contradictions, and human-like capacity for making catastrophically bad decisions.

This is not a religion of distant, perfect beings. These gods bleed, scheme, fall in love, lose, grieve, and die. That is part of why they still resonate — not as objects of worship so much as mirrors, reflecting back something honest about what it means to be alive in a world that does not always cooperate.

As for modern practitioners: no, they are not raiding monasteries. The Norse Pagans alive today — and there are more of them than you might expect — find meaning in nature, in community, in the old stories retold on their own terms. They are farmers and software engineers and students who happen to light a bonfire on the summer solstice and raise a horn to Odin. We will meet them properly later in the book.

For now, set aside whatever image of Vikings your favorite television show has given you, set aside the horned helmets that actual Vikings never wore, and come with me. There is a great deal more to this story than most people realize.

Skol.

Chapter One

The Origins of Norse Paganism

Cast your mind back to 10,000 B.C.E. The Ice Age is ending. Scandinavia — not yet called that, not yet called anything — is beginning to thaw, and the first people are arriving on land that has never been farmed, hunted, or named. The evidence they left behind is thin: a few tools, a handful of burial sites, the faint outline of lives lived at the very edge of survival. From this period all the way to roughly 500 B.C.E., the historical record is more silence than story.

This is worth sitting with for a moment. Everything we think we know about ancient Norse belief rests on evidence — archaeological findings, later literary sources, comparative mythology — and not on any firsthand account written by the people themselves. The further back we go, the more we are reading the past through shadows. This does not make the history less fascinating. It makes it more so. We are detectives working a very cold case.

The Sami People

Among the first groups to settle the Scandinavian peninsula were the Sami — an indigenous people who arrived sometime between 10,000 and 5,000 B.C.E., spreading across present-day Norway, Sweden, Finland, and the Kola Peninsula of Russia. They were not the ancestors of the Norse in any direct genetic sense, but they were their neighbors, and for centuries the two peoples lived in contact close enough that ideas, beliefs, and practices passed freely between them.

The Sami are still with us today. Statistics Norway estimated their population in 2011 at around 37,890 within Norway alone, with communities scattered across Scandinavia and diaspora populations as far as the United States and Ukraine. They are one of Europe's few surviving indigenous groups with an unbroken cultural thread stretching back to the Stone Age — which makes them an extraordinary window into a world that would otherwise be entirely lost.

In those earliest centuries, the Sami lived as hunter-gatherers in one of the harshest climates on earth. Their tools were hammerstones, bone points, antler blades — instruments refined over generations into axes, spears, and scrapers capable of sustaining life through Scandinavian winters that would have defeated most people. Every day was a negotiation with the land: what it would give, what it would withhold, and what might be done to tip the balance.

It is precisely under these conditions — where a failed hunt or a brutal winter could mean the death of an entire community — that the Sami developed a spiritual life of remarkable sophistication.

Three Pillars of Belief

The religion of the early Sami was built on three interlocking foundations: animism, polytheism, and shamanism.

Animism is the belief that the natural world is alive in ways that go beyond biology — that animals, rivers, rocks, and forests contain spirits with their own consciousness and will. For people whose survival depended entirely on nature's cooperation, this was not a poetic idea. It was a practical one. A hunter who believed the elk he was tracking had a spirit worth respecting would approach it differently — and perhaps more successfully — than one who did not. The world was not a collection of inert resources to be exploited. It was a community of beings to be negotiated with.

Polytheism — the belief in multiple gods and divine powers — would become one of the defining features of Norse Paganism centuries later. Among the Sami it appeared early, in a shifting pantheon of nature spirits, weather beings, and ancestor figures whose names and characters varied by region and season. There was no single authority, no creator god standing apart from creation and directing it from above. Instead, power was distributed across the landscape itself, resident in particular places, particular animals, particular forces that the Sami had learned to identify and address over generations.

Shamanism was the mechanism through which these beliefs were enacted. A shaman — in Sami, a *noaidi* — was the community's specialist in navigating the boundary between the visible world and the spirit world. The noaidi healed the sick, guided the souls of the dead toward the afterlife, predicted the movements of animals, and interceded with supernatural forces on behalf of the living. These were not ceremonial roles. In a world without medicine, without meteorology, without any reliable way of predicting whether the next season would bring abundance or famine, the noaidi's function was as load-bearing as the hunter's or the farmer's.

The Noaidi

The noaidi occupied a position in Sami society that was at once necessary and unsettling. They were respected, sometimes feared, occasionally resented — figures whose access to hidden knowledge made them enormously valuable and, by the same token, genuinely uncanny. Set apart from the community by what they knew and what they could do, they were never entirely subject to the normal rules that governed everyone else.

Becoming a noaidi was not a matter of appointment or inheritance, though families with a tradition of practice had an advantage. It required years of learning — the development of specific skills, the cultivation of relationships with specific spirits, the accumulation of experience in territories of consciousness that most people never approached. The training was demanding in ways that went beyond the physical, and the accounts that survive suggest it could be genuinely dangerous, not in a bodily sense but psychologically. A noaidi was someone who had learned to move through the landscape of the spirit world and return from it intact. Not everyone who attempted it succeeded.

Both men and women could become noaidi, which distinguished the Sami tradition from many of the religious structures that would later replace it. The Christianity that eventually reached Scandinavia had clear and consistent views about which gender could hold religious authority. The Sami tradition did not share those views, and this openness left traces in what would become Norse Paganism — particularly in the figure of the völva, the Norse seeress whose practice closely mirrored the noaidi's, and who occupied a similarly ambiguous position of power and social otherness.

The Drum as a Map

The primary tools of the noaidi were rhythm and song, and the most important physical object in their practice was the drum.

Sami ritual drums were not simply percussion instruments. They were cosmological documents. The surface of each drum — typically made from reindeer skin stretched over a carved wooden frame — was painted with figures representing the spirit world: gods, animals, paths between realms, the sun, the moon, sacred mountains and rivers. No two drums were identical. Each one was a personal map, built over years to reflect the specific spiritual terrain its owner had learned to navigate.

During a ritual, the noaidi would beat the drum in sustained, repetitive patterns while chanting — a combination that gradually shifted consciousness away from the ordinary world and toward the altered state in which spirit contact became possible. The drum's imagery served as orientation during the journey: a visual anchor that told the noaidi where they were in territory invisible to everyone else in the room. When we look at these drums today in Scandinavian museums, we are looking at something that functioned simultaneously as a musical instrument, a sacred text, and a navigation chart for the invisible world.

The scholar Alan Holloway describes two distinct modes of spirit travel that the noaidi practiced. In the first, the "free soul" left the body entirely and moved through the spirit world under its own power — a full departure that required the deepest trance state and the greatest skill to manage safely. In the second, the "body soul" remained tethered to the physical world, perceiving the spirit realm without fully crossing into it — a kind of supervised vision rather than a complete journey. Both states required the drum, the chant, and the years of training that made the difference between navigation and getting lost.

We have records of shamanic practice from human cultures going back at least 40,000 years, making it one of the oldest documented religious behaviors in human history. Among the Sami, it took a form uniquely shaped by the landscape they inhabited — immense, cold, dark for months at a stretch, populated by animals whose behavior could mean the difference between survival and starvation. The drums reflect this landscape. The spirits they navigate are the spirits of exactly this kind of world.

A Vision of the Afterlife

The Sami concept of the afterlife was called *saivo*, and it deserves more attention than it usually receives, because it anticipates something we will encounter again much later in this book.

Saivo was not a place of judgment. There were no scales, no accounting of sins, no eternal punishment waiting for those who had lived imperfectly. It was instead a mirror of the world the living inhabited — but corrected. In saivo, game was plentiful. Shelter was adequate. The cold was manageable. The harsh negotiations with an uncooperative landscape that defined daily life in the physical world were replaced by a version of existence in which the land cooperated. For people who spent their entire lives in genuine scarcity, this was not a modest promise. It was the most radical possible improvement on every condition they actually knew.

The noaidi's relationship with saivo was active rather than passive. The dead were not simply mourned and left behind. They remained available — sources of guidance, warning, and memory that the living could access through the right rituals and the right practitioners. Ancestors were consulted about hunts, about disputes, about the intentions of the spirits that governed weather and animal movement. Death was a transition, not an ending, and the boundary between the living and the dead was something a skilled noaidi could cross in both directions.

The echo of all this in what would later become Norse Paganism is impossible to miss. Valhalla — the Norse hall of the slain, where the honored dead feast and train for the final battle — is saivo translated into a warrior culture's terms: the same fundamental promise of continuation, the same active relationship between the living and the dead, the same understanding that what comes after life is not a void but a place with its own conditions and its own inhabitants. The Norse seeresses who could speak with the dead were practicing something structurally identical to what the Sami noaidi had been doing for thousands of years before the first Viking ever put to sea.

Two Peoples, One Landscape

By the time the North Germanic peoples arrived in Scandinavia and began developing what we would eventually recognize as Norse culture, the Sami had already been there for millennia, working out a relationship with this landscape and its invisible inhabitants.

What followed was not conquest or erasure but something more complex and more interesting: centuries of contact, trade, intermarriage, and cultural exchange in the borderlands where the two peoples met. Norse sagas mention the Sami repeatedly — sometimes as figures of fear and mystery, sometimes as sources of magical knowledge that the Norse admired and occasionally tried to acquire, occasionally as allies or trading partners. Sami shamanic practices appear in Norse accounts with a familiarity that suggests ongoing contact rather than exotic novelty.

The Norse god Odin himself, as we will discover in later chapters, shares a startling number of characteristics with the Sami noaidi: the staff, the trance, the journeys between worlds, the ravens that carry information from the far reaches of the cosmos, the willingness to pay catastrophic personal prices for hidden knowledge. Whether Odin's mythology was directly shaped by contact with Sami practice, or whether both traditions drew independently from the same deep well of shamanic thinking that stretches back tens of thousands of years, is a question that scholars continue to work through.

What seems clear is that the two traditions were in conversation for long enough that separating them cleanly is probably impossible — and may not even be the right ambition.

What we can say is this: when we look for the deepest roots of what the Vikings believed, we are led not to the Viking Age itself — not to its longships and raids and famous battles — but here, to this much older and quieter tradition, in the hands of a people reading the spirit world in a drumbeat long before anyone thought to carve a ship from a Scandinavian forest.

The drums have mostly fallen silent now. But the world they mapped is still there — in the stories, in the rituals, in the names of the gods, in the structure of a cosmology that understood the visible world as the thinnest layer of a reality that extended, in all directions, much further than the eye could reach.

That is where this book begins.

CHAPTER TWO

The Bronze and Iron Age

Five thousand years ago, someone in Scandinavia buried a small bronze razor in the ground alongside the body of a man they had loved or honored or feared. We found it. We have found thousands of objects like it — blades, brooches, belt buckles, arm rings, the occasional sword — each one a message sent forward through time by people who had no idea anyone would ever receive it.

The Bronze Age is where the archaeological record begins to speak clearly, and what it tells us is surprising. These were not isolated barbarians scratching at frozen earth in ignorance of the wider world. They were participants in one of the most extensive trade networks the ancient world ever produced, exchanging goods with civilizations thousands of miles away, absorbing foreign ideas, and developing a material culture sophisticated enough to leave behind objects that still stop people in their tracks in museums today.

From Stone to Metal

The transition from the Stone Age to the Bronze Age was not a single event but a slow revolution that spread across the world at different speeds, depending on geography, available resources, and contact with other cultures. The ancient Sumerians of the Middle East were among the first to work with bronze, combining copper and tin to produce a metal harder and more versatile than either component alone. Some Greek civilizations made the transition before 3,000 B.C.E. China followed considerably later, around 1,900 to 1,600 B.C.E.

Scandinavia entered the Bronze Age around 1,800 B.C.E. — later than the Mediterranean world, earlier than some might expect. The reason for the delay was geological: the Scandinavian peninsula had almost no copper or tin of its own. Bronze could not be produced locally. It had to be acquired through trade, which meant that entering the Bronze Age required first building the relationships that made trade possible.

What Scandinavia did have was amber.

The Amber Trade

Amber — fossilized tree resin, golden and translucent, warm to the touch in a way that stone never is — was found in abundance along the Baltic coastline, particularly in Denmark, which became the primary hub of Scandinavian trade during this period. To the civilizations of the Mediterranean and the Middle East, amber was extraordinary: exotic, beautiful, and charged with a mysterious static electricity that led some to believe it had supernatural properties. It turned up in Egyptian tombs. It was traded as far as Anatolia. It was buried with the wealthy dead from one end of the ancient world to the other.

In exchange for amber, Scandinavians received bronze — the raw material that would transform their society. Denmark was the gateway through which these transactions passed, and the trade routes that developed stretched from the Baltic Sea south through the river systems of Europe all the way to the Mediterranean. Along these routes moved not just goods but languages, technologies, and religious ideas. The world was smaller than it looked.

These routes also carried something less tangible but equally important: prestige. Owning an object that had traveled a great distance was a statement. A bronze blade from the south, a piece of amber jewelry crafted in a foreign style, a drinking vessel made by hands that had never seen the Baltic — these things communicated connections, relationships, access to a wider world.

The chiefs and elites of Bronze Age Scandinavia understood this perfectly, and they accumulated imported objects with the same deliberate attention that later rulers would devote to armies and fortifications.

It is worth pausing on what this means. By the time Rome was founded in 753 B.C.E., Scandinavian traders had already been operating within a continental network for more than a thousand years. The Greeks and Romans who later wrote of northern Europeans as primitive barbarians were describing people who had been in commercial contact with the civilized world since before Greece itself existed in any recognizable form. The condescension was, to put it gently, not entirely warranted.

What Bronze Made Possible

Once bronze began flowing into Scandinavia, everything changed. Weapons became sharper and more durable. Tools became more precise. Jewelry became more elaborate. And with material wealth came the social stratification that always follows it — the emergence of elites, of chieftains, of people wealthy enough to commission fine objects and powerful enough to demand they be buried with them.

The burial mounds of Bronze Age Scandinavia are among the richest sources we have for understanding this period, and what they reveal is a society already developing the religious sensibility that would eventually become Norse Paganism. Objects were buried not merely for practical reasons but as offerings — gifts to deities, provisions for the afterlife, statements about the status and beliefs of the dead. The care taken in these burials was extraordinary. Bodies were wrapped, dressed, accompanied. The dead were not simply disposed of. They were seen off.

The burial goods also tell us something about gender roles in this society. Men were typically interred with weapons — swords, razors, tools of war and grooming that spoke to a public, physical role in the world. Women were buried with clothing items, bronze belts worn around the waist, and jewelry: brooches, arm rings, decorative pins. Both were buried with considerable attention to detail, suggesting that the afterlife was imagined as a continuation of the life that preceded it, requiring the same equipment and the same social markers. This is a belief we will encounter again and again as we move deeper into Norse Paganism — the idea that death does not reset a person to zero, but carries them forward, with their identity and their possessions intact, into whatever comes next.

The Sun Chariot

Among all the objects the Bronze Age left behind in Scandinavia, one stands apart.

The Trundholm Sun Chariot, discovered in Denmark in 1902, dates to around 1,400 B.C.E. It is a bronze model of a horse pulling a large disc on a wheeled platform — the disc itself coated on one side with a thin layer of hammered gold. When we look at it today, in the National Museum of Denmark in Copenhagen, we are looking at a theological statement. The sun, in the belief system of Bronze Age Scandinavians, was not simply a natural phenomenon. It was divine, and it moved across the sky because something was pulling it.

The horse, domesticated in Scandinavia sometime in the second millennium B.C.E., held enormous symbolic weight. Its introduction into Scandinavian culture coincided with a period of rapid change — new agricultural methods, new social structures, new religious ideas — and the Sun Chariot captures the moment when these threads came together. Here is a god-horse, drawing the light of the world on its daily journey. Here, in miniature, is an entire cosmology.

It is not difficult to trace the line from this object to the elaborate mythology about the sun, the sky, and the divine horses of later Norse religion. These ideas had deep roots, and the Trundholm chariot is evidence that they were already fully formed a thousand years before the Viking Age began.

The Collapse and What Came After

Around 1,200 B.C.E., the Bronze Age ended — not gracefully, but in something close to catastrophe. Across the Mediterranean and the Near East, the great Bronze Age civilizations collapsed within a period of decades:

palaces burned, trade routes dissolved, populations displaced. Historians still debate the cause. Climate change, famine, internal rebellions, invasions by the peoples the Egyptians called the Sea Peoples — most likely some combination of all of these. What is clear is that the disruption was severe enough to fundamentally reorganize the ancient world.

For Scandinavia, the collapse of the Mediterranean trade network meant the end of the amber-for-bronze exchange. Bronze became scarce. The material that had defined Scandinavian culture for over a thousand years was suddenly difficult to obtain, and a replacement was needed.

That replacement was iron.

The Iron Age

Iron is harder to work than bronze. It requires higher temperatures to smelt, more skill to shape, and more labor to maintain. But it has one overwhelming advantage: it is everywhere. Bronze requires specific geological conditions and a functioning trade network. Iron ore is found in bogs, in swamps, in the ordinary ground beneath ordinary fields. For a society cut off from its Mediterranean suppliers, this mattered enormously.

Scandinavia entered the Iron Age around 500 B.C.E. — later than Greece or the Near East, but for reasons that made geographical sense. This gap is itself worth noting. In Italy, the Iron Age effectively ended with Roman conquest, somewhere around the second or first century B.C.E. In Scandinavia, it lasted until approximately 800 C.E. — nearly a thousand years longer. An age that had already closed in the Mediterranean world before the birth of Christ was still actively shaping Scandinavian life well into the ninth century. This is a reminder that historical periods are not universal but local, defined not by calendar dates but by the conditions of each society. The Norse were not behind. They were simply operating on different terms, in a different landscape, with different resources and different pressures.

Once the transition to iron happened, it happened on entirely local terms. Scandinavian iron was smelted from bog iron ore — deposits formed naturally in the low-oxygen conditions of peatlands, requiring no mining infrastructure, no imported raw materials, no external relationships. For the first time,

Scandinavians could produce the metal they needed entirely from their own land. The self-sufficiency this created was not just economic. It was psychological. A people who had spent centuries dependent on distant trade networks now had what they needed underfoot.

The social consequences were significant. Communities that had depended on trade for their most important materials became more self-reliant. Agricultural settlements grew larger and more organized. The labor that had previously gone into maintaining trade relationships went instead into farming, building, and the development of increasingly sophisticated local crafts. Slavery, relatively rare in the Bronze Age, began to play a more prominent role as communities needed additional labor for agricultural expansion — a development that would continue and intensify into the Viking Age.

The Iron Age is also, for historians, a period of dramatically improved visibility. Bronze Age Scandinavia is rich in objects but thin in written records. The Iron Age gives us more: inscriptions, carvings, artifacts with discernible symbolic content that can be connected to the religious ideas we find described in much later Norse literature. The gods begin to take shape. The cosmological thinking that will eventually produce the Eddas starts to leave traces in the material record. We are still reading shadows, but the shadows are getting sharper.

The Iron Age in Scandinavia lasted from roughly 500 B.C.E. until around 800 C.E. — the point at which a young monk on a small island off the coast of Northumbria would look up from his work and see, to his horror, the first Viking ships coming in from the sea.

That story is next.

Chapter Three

The Viking Age

Before we talk about the Vikings themselves — their farms and their raids, their ships and their gods — we need to talk about how we know any of it.

This is not a minor point. The Viking Age is the most visible period in Norse history, the one most people arrive with preconceptions about, and yet the evidence on which our understanding rests is thinner and more complicated than most people realize. The further we go back in time, as we have already seen, the more we are reading the past through incomplete and often contradictory sources. The Viking Age is no exception. What we know — and what we think we know — comes from a specific set of documents, each with its own limitations, and from the patient work of archaeologists who have spent the last two centuries digging up what the documents left out.

The Sources

The most important literary sources for Norse Paganism were not written during the Viking Age. They were written after it, by people who were already living in a Christianized world, and they carry the fingerprints of that transformation on every page.

The Poetic Edda is a collection of Old Norse poems composed anonymously by multiple authors, written down sometime in the thirteenth century but drawing on oral traditions that are considerably older. Two poems in particular have become foundational texts for anyone trying to understand Norse cosmology. The first, *Völuspá* — "The Insight of the Seeress" — is a sweeping account of the creation of the world and its eventual destruction at Ragnarök, narrated by a völva, a seeress, who has been summoned by Odin himself to tell him what she knows. The second, *Grímnismál* — "The Song of the Hooded One" — is Odin speaking in disguise, describing the nine worlds and the halls of the gods in meticulous, sometimes baffling detail. Both poems are extraordinary. Both were written down by Christians, which means we can never be entirely sure how much the original material was edited, softened, or subtly reframed.

The Prose Edda is a different kind of document entirely. Written around 1220 by an Icelander named Snorri Sturluson — poet, politician, historian, and one of the most remarkable figures of the medieval Norse world — it is not a collection of sacred texts but a manual. Sturluson wrote the Prose Edda as a guide to skaldic poetry, the highly formalized verse tradition of the Norse courts, which was full of mythological references that were already becoming obscure by his time. To explain the poetry, he had to explain the mythology behind it, and the result is the most comprehensive account of Norse belief that survives. The Prose Edda is divided into four sections: a Prologue in which Sturluson, a Christian, attempts to rationalize the Norse gods as legendary human kings rather than actual deities; *Gylfaginning*, a detailed account of Norse mythology structured as a dialogue; *Skáldskaparmál*, an extended discussion of poetic language and kennings; and *Háttatal*, a treatise on verse forms.

Sturluson's Prose Edda is invaluable and problematic in roughly equal measure. Without it, our knowledge of Norse mythology would be fragmentary at best. With it, we have a detailed and coherent account — but one filtered through the mind of a thirteenth-century Christian intellectual who had his own interpretive agenda and who was working, in some cases, from sources we no longer have.

Then there are the Sagas — prose narratives written in the thirteenth and fourteenth centuries, describing the lives of Icelandic settlers, Scandinavian kings, and legendary heroes. The Sagas treat Norse Paganism differently from the Eddas: casually, in passing, as background rather than subject. A character might make an offering to Thor before a sea voyage without the text pausing to explain what that means or why. This casualness is actually part of what makes the Sagas useful — they give us glimpses of how religious practice was embedded in ordinary life, rather than presenting it as doctrine. One exception is the *Ynglinga Saga*, also written by Sturluson, which treats the Norse gods as historical kings whose deeds were later mythologized — an approach that tells us something interesting about how a medieval Icelander made sense of his own heritage.

Alongside all of this literature sits the archaeological record, and it is in many ways the most reliable source we have. Objects do not have agendas. A buried ship does not have a theological position. The grave goods, the runestones, the settlement patterns, the bog finds — these things confirm, complicate, and occasionally contradict what the texts tell us, and they do so without any of the literary filtering that makes the Eddas and Sagas so difficult to read at face value.

Our understanding of the Viking Age is, as a result, genuinely incomplete. We are working with pieces of a puzzle whose full image we will never see. What we can do is be honest about which pieces we have, which ones are missing, and which ones might be showing us something slightly different from what they appear to show.

With that said — here are the Vikings.

Life on the Farm

Forget the longships for a moment. Forget the raids, the helmets, the battle-axes. The overwhelming majority of people who lived in Viking Age Scandinavia spent their entire lives doing something far less dramatic: farming.

Norse society was organized around the rural farmstead. Families lived in longhouses — long, low timber structures with few windows, their interiors lit by candles and oil lamps, warmed by a central hearth whose smoke rose through a hole in the roof. Wealthier households had separate buildings for storage, livestock, and workshops. Poorer families shared their single room with whatever animals needed shelter during the winter. The smell, the noise, and the intimacy of this existence are not easy to imagine from the outside.

Work was divided along strict gender lines, though the division was less about hierarchy than about the different kinds of expertise each role demanded. Men handled the outdoor agricultural labor: plowing, sowing, harvesting, maintaining tools, managing livestock in the fields. Women ran the household economy: producing cloth, preserving food, brewing beer and mead, managing the dairy animals, and overseeing the domestic operations that kept the family fed and clothed through a Scandinavian winter. Neither role was marginal. In an environment where a bad harvest or a poorly preserved food supply could mean starvation, the women's work was as load-bearing as the men's.

The staple crops were barley, oats, and rye. Plowing was done with a wooden ard — a basic scratch plow that broke the surface of the soil but did not turn it, requiring fields to be plowed twice in perpendicular directions to be effective. The iron plow, which would have made this work considerably easier, did not arrive in Scandinavia until after the Viking Age had ended. In the meantime, the plowing was done by hand, by ox, by horse, and in households wealthy enough to own them, by slaves.

Slavery was a feature of Viking Age society that modern popular culture tends to gloss over. Thralls — enslaved people — were acquired primarily through raids, sold at markets, and put to work on the most physically punishing and degrading tasks the farm required: spreading manure, breaking ground, building and repairing structures. Their legal status was essentially that of property. How they were treated depended entirely on the character of the person who owned them, and accounts from the period suggest the range ran from brutal to merely grim.

The physical reality of Viking life was considerably harder than its popular image suggests. The skeletons recovered from Viking Age burial sites tell a corrective story: people who showed the effects of heavy labor, chronic malnutrition, and diseases that killed them young. The historian Anders Winroth, in *The Age of the Vikings*, notes that the familiar image of the Viking as a large, strong, physically imposing figure needs to be set against the archaeological evidence of actual Viking Age bodies, which often tell a different story. Just under half of all children did not survive to adulthood. Famine was not a distant threat but a recurring reality. This was not a comfortable world.

Beyond the Horizon

What drove people out of this hard, familiar world and onto the open sea?

The question of Viking motivation has occupied historians for generations, and the honest answer is that it was not one thing. The popular theory — that Scandinavia was running out of resources and the raids were a response to scarcity — does not hold up well under scrutiny. The population was not large enough to have exhausted the land, and the Norse were already experienced traders who had other ways of obtaining what they needed. Resource scarcity alone does not explain why a farmer's son decided to get into a boat and sail toward England.

What does explain it, at least in part, is the same thing that has driven young men toward violence and adventure in every culture and every era: reputation. Viking society placed enormous weight on a man's name — his standing in the community, his honor, the stories told about him by people who would outlive him. Wealth was not simply comfortable. Wealth was the material proof of a man's worth, and the way wealth translated into status, influence, and the favor of the gods. A chieftain who could distribute silver and land to his followers attracted more followers, which meant more successful raids, which meant more silver and land. The system was self-reinforcing, and it rewarded aggression.

There was also land. England, in particular, offered something that large parts of Scandinavia could not: soft, deep, hospitable soil that would grow crops with a generosity the northern climate rarely permitted. For settlers willing to take the risk, an English field was not just an economic opportunity — it was a transformation of their material circumstances. The Vikings understood this, and sometimes they did not even have to fight for it. Terrified communities offered tribute — land, silver, hostages — in exchange for the promise that the raiders would move on. The Vikings understood negotiation as well as they understood violence, and they used both with a pragmatism that their enemies found particularly unnerving.

Erik the Red and the Edge of the World

No story illustrates the Viking relationship with exploration and exile better than that of Erik the Red, the man who discovered Greenland — largely because he had run out of places to be expelled from.

Erik was born in Rogaland, Norway, around 950 C.E., the son of a man who had himself been banished from Norway for manslaughter. The family had settled in Iceland, where Erik promptly continued the tradition. His thralls caused a landslide on a neighboring farm. The neighbor hired a man to kill them. Erik killed the man. He was exiled from his district for three years. During that exile, he lent some inherited heirlooms to a man named Thorgest. When his exile ended and he returned to collect them, the heirlooms were gone. He took Thorgest's possessions instead. Thorgest's sons came after him. Erik killed them. The Icelanders exiled him for another three years.

It was during this second exile — adrift, unwelcome, with nowhere obvious to go — that Erik sailed west and found Greenland.

What he found was not quite what he later described to potential settlers. The western coast was not uninhabitable — there were areas where conditions allowed for farming and where the sea provided plentiful walrus, seal, and whale. But it was considerably colder than Iceland, and describing it accurately would not have attracted the kind of enthusiastic colonists he needed. So he called it Greenland, spoke of its possibilities with great enthusiasm, and managed to assemble a fleet of twenty-five ships. Fourteen reached their destination. The rest turned back or were lost.

The settlers established two communities on the western and eastern coasts, separated by roughly four hundred miles of ice. They survived, traded, and prospered modestly for several centuries, using the marine resources of the Greenlandic coast to acquire European goods they could not produce themselves. They also pushed further west — and it was from Greenland that Leif Erikson, Erik's son, eventually made the crossing to North America, roughly five hundred years before Columbus sailed.

By the time of the Greenland settlement, Christianity was already spreading through Scandinavia. Erik remained loyal to the old gods throughout his life. His wife converted, and according to the sagas, expressed her devotion by refusing to sleep with him — a detail that the sources record with a matter-of-factness that suggests no one found it particularly surprising.

The Raids

On June 8, 793 C.E., Viking ships appeared off the coast of Lindisfarne — a small, tidal island off the northeast coast of England, home to one of the most important Christian monasteries in the British Isles.

What followed was not the first Viking raid on British shores. There had been earlier attacks on settlements in Wessex and Mercia. But Lindisfarne was different in scale, in symbolism, and in the terror it produced. The monastery was not a military target. It was a center of learning and religious life, its monks engaged in the slow, precise work of illuminating manuscripts and preserving knowledge. It was also, like most monasteries of the period, largely undefended and full of valuable objects. The Vikings destroyed it with a thoroughness that shocked Europe.

The Anglo-Saxon Chronicle describes the approach of the attack in terms that reveal how completely the Vikings exceeded the imaginative categories of those they attacked — preceded by whirlwinds, lightning, and "fiery dragons" seen flying in the air. These were not meteorological observations. They were the language of people trying to make sense of something that felt genuinely apocalyptic. The historian Else Roesdahl's account, drawing on the Chronicle, captures the atmosphere: portents in the sky, famine as a sign of divine displeasure, and then the raiders themselves, arriving from the sea like a punishment.

Simeon of Durham, writing in the twelfth century, described what the Vikings actually did: plundering the treasury, desecrating the altars, dragging monks away in chains, drowning others in the sea. The scholar Alcuin of York, who was in Charlemagne's court at the time, wrote to the King of Northumbria that the church had been "spattered with the blood of the priests of God" — a phrase that communicated not just horror but genuine theological bewilderment. How could God have allowed his house to be violated in this way?

The Vikings had a simple answer, though they were not asked for it: the monastery was wealthy, it was unguarded, and it was there.

This is worth understanding clearly. The attack on Lindisfarne was not motivated by hatred of Christianity. The Vikings had no particular interest in suppressing a foreign religion, and in the years that followed, many of them would adopt that religion themselves when it suited them politically. Churches and monasteries were targeted because they were where the valuable things were kept — silver crosses, illuminated manuscripts with jeweled covers, the accumulated donations of generations of wealthy patrons — and because the people inside them were not soldiers. It was ruthlessly logical.

The raids that followed Lindisfarne spread across the British Isles, into the Frankish Empire, down the rivers of Eastern Europe into Byzantium and the Islamic world, and eventually to North America. The Frankish response eventually produced one of the more striking diplomatic arrangements of the era: the Viking chieftain Rollo was given the region we now call Normandy in exchange for his agreement to stop raiding the Franks, protect the local population, and convert to Christianity. Rollo agreed. His descendants would eventually become the Normans, and one of them — William the Conqueror — would invade England in 1066, changing the course of European history in ways that no one in a Viking longship could have anticipated.

The chieftains who organized these raids operated within a system that Winroth describes with elegant clarity: reputation, generosity, and violence were not separate forces but a single interconnected economy. A chieftain needed victories to acquire wealth. He needed wealth to be generous to his men. His generosity attracted more men, which produced more victories. Poets celebrated successful chieftains, which spread their fame, which attracted yet more warriors. The system rewarded escalation and punished caution, and it produced some of the most effective military forces the early medieval world had seen.

It also, eventually, produced its own end. The world the Vikings were raiding was changing around them — consolidating into larger kingdoms, building better defenses, developing the political and military structures that would make the old raiding economy increasingly unviable. The Viking Age did not end with a single defeat or a decisive moment. It dissolved, gradually, into the world that came after it.

That world was Christian. How Scandinavia got there is the subject of the next chapter.

Chapter Four

The Christianization of Scandinavia

Religions do not usually die in battle. They erode — slowly, unevenly, across generations — as the conditions that sustained them shift and the people who practiced them find new arrangements more convenient, more profitable, or simply more inevitable. The end of Norse Paganism as the dominant belief system of Scandinavia was not a conquest. It was a negotiation, drawn out over roughly a hundred and fifty years, conducted simultaneously on political, economic, and spiritual terms, and never quite completed in the way the Christians who drove it would have liked to believe.

The story of how Scandinavia became Christian is, in many ways, more interesting than the story of how it stayed pagan. It tells us something about how people actually change their minds — or decide not to — when the stakes are high enough.

The Economics of Conversion

To understand why the Norse converted, it helps to set aside the idea that religious conversion is primarily a spiritual event. For most of the chieftains and kings who led Scandinavia's transition to Christianity, the calculation was considerably more pragmatic.

By the ninth and tenth centuries, the trade networks of northern Europe were increasingly controlled by Christian powers. The Frankish Empire, the Byzantine court, the Anglo-Saxon kingdoms — all of them operated within a Christian framework that extended, in practical terms, to commercial relationships. A Norse merchant who wanted to do business in a Frankish city needed to demonstrate, at minimum, a credible association with the Christian world. This did not necessarily require genuine belief. It required the right signs.

Viking traders began accepting a ritual called *prima signatio* — a preliminary marking with the sign of the cross that fell short of full baptism but was enough to signal that they were at least open to Christian influence. It was a kind of commercial compromise: the traders kept their access to Christian markets, the Christians kept their sense that the heathens were moving in the right direction, and no one had to commit to anything they found inconvenient. It was, in its way, thoroughly Norse in spirit — pragmatic, flexible, oriented toward outcomes rather than abstractions.

Full baptism, when it came, brought more tangible rewards. In Frankish society, newly baptized Norse leaders received fine garments, gifts, and political recognition from their sponsors — usually powerful Christian nobles who gained, in return, a useful ally and the spiritual credit of having brought another soul into the faith. The exchange was understood by both sides to be partly transactional, and this did not seem to trouble anyone particularly.

Harald Bluetooth and the Jelling Stones

The most dramatically documented conversion in Scandinavian history belongs to Harald Bluetooth, King of Denmark, who ruled from roughly 958 to 986 C.E. and whose name, improbably, now lives on in every wireless device on the planet.

Harald's conversion to Christianity is commemorated on one of the most remarkable objects to survive from the Viking Age: the large runestone at Jelling, in central Denmark. The stone — carved sometime around 965, decorated with an image of Christ intertwined with organic knotwork, and bearing an inscription in runic script — declares that Harald "made the Danes Christian." It is the nearest thing Scandinavia produced to an official proclamation of religious change, and it is worth noting that it was written in runes, the sacred alphabet of the old religion, on a stone that stands alongside two enormous burial mounds associated with Harald's pagan ancestors.

The coexistence of these elements — Christian imagery, runic script, ancestral pagan monuments — is not an accident or a contradiction. It is a portrait of how conversion actually worked. Harald did not demolish the old mounds. He built his Christian statement alongside them, in the same sacred space, in a gesture that could be read as continuity rather than rupture. Whether this was theological sophistication or political calculation is a question that probably did not feel distinct to Harald himself.

The physical evidence from the period around the Jelling stones reinforces this picture of coexistence. A soapstone mold found in Himmerland, Denmark — used to cast small metal objects — contains the forms for both Christian crosses and Thor's hammers. The same craftsman was producing religious objects for both faiths simultaneously, serving a population that had not yet decided, or did not feel it needed to decide, between them. This is not syncretism as a philosophical position. It is pragmatism as a way of life.

The Logic of Polytheism

One reason the conversion took as long as it did — and remained as incomplete as it did — is that Norse Paganism was structurally better equipped than Christianity to absorb a new deity without crisis.

A monotheistic religion requires the rejection of all competing gods. The Christian God does not share the category of "god" with anyone else; believing in him means, by definition, not believing in Odin or Thor. But a polytheist operates in a world already full of divine beings with different domains and different levels of relevance to different situations. Adding the Christian God to that world was not, from a Norse perspective, a theological problem. It was an expansion of the available resources.

The Icelandic *Landnámabók* records a settler named Helgi the Lean who is described as believing in Christ — but who, when faced with storms at sea, called on Thor. This is often cited as an example of incomplete conversion, of a man caught between two worlds. But it might be more accurate to read it as a man operating within a perfectly coherent logic: the Christian God handled some things, Thor handled others, and a sensible person used the right tool for the situation. The missionaries who found this attitude maddening were applying a standard of religious exclusivity that the Norse had never lived by and saw no particular reason to adopt.

This flexibility also meant that the conflict between the old religion and the new was rarely as sharp in practice as the Christian sources liked to present it. The missionaries sent to convert Scandinavia encountered genuine resistance — particularly when they demanded not just the acceptance of Christ but the active abandonment of the old gods, which felt to many Norse people like an act of ingratitude toward powers that had protected and sustained their families for generations. Some of the restrictions the church tried to impose made the tension concrete: the prohibition on eating horse meat struck at a practice with deep ritual significance in Norse culture, and the demand that parents not expose unwanted newborns challenged customs that, however brutal by modern standards, were embedded in the economic logic of survival in a hard environment.

But outright religious warfare was rare. The conversion of Scandinavia produced skirmishes and resentments and considerable passive noncompliance, not crusades. At least, not yet.

The Kings Who Converted by Force

If Harald Bluetooth represents the diplomatic face of Scandinavian Christianization, the two Olafs represent something considerably less gentle.

Olaf Tryggvason became King of Norway in 995 C.E. after a career as a Viking raider that had taken him as far as England and Ireland, where he had encountered Christianity and, apparently, found it convincing. He returned to Norway a genuine believer — or at least a man whose belief and political ambition pointed in exactly the same direction — and proceeded to Christianize his kingdom with a thoroughness that left little room for dissent. Temples were destroyed. Priests of the old religion were killed, driven out, or forced to convert. Communities that resisted found themselves facing military consequences. Olaf understood, correctly, that centralized Christian kingship and the distributed power of the old pagan chieftains were incompatible, and he acted accordingly.

His successor, Olaf Haraldsson — later canonized as Saint Olaf, patron saint of Norway — continued in much the same vein after taking the throne in 1015. Where Tryggvason had been forceful, Haraldsson was systematic. He imported English clergy, built churches on the sites of pagan temples, and worked to replace the legal and social framework of the old religion with Christian institutions. He was killed in battle in 1030 at Stiklestad, fighting Norwegian chieftains who had allied with the Danish king Cnut — a coalition in which the defense of the old ways was tangled up with straightforward political resistance to royal centralization. Miracles were reported at his tomb almost immediately, and his canonization followed with unusual speed. The man who had been killed by his own people became their most important saint within a generation, which tells you something about how quickly the religious landscape was shifting.

What both Olafs understood, and what their methods reveal, is that the conversion of Scandinavia was never purely a matter of individual conscience. It was a restructuring of power, conducted under religious cover, and opposed by people who grasped exactly what was at stake.

Iceland's Democratic Conversion

Not every corner of Scandinavia converted at sword point. Iceland's path to Christianity is one of the strangest and most revealing episodes in the entire story — a negotiated settlement that preserved the old religion in private even as it abolished it in public.

Iceland had been settled in the late ninth century largely by Norse emigrants fleeing the consolidating power of Harald Fairhair, the first king to unite Norway under a single rule. It was governed not by a king but by the Althing — an annual assembly of chieftains and free farmers that served as parliament, law court, and social gathering simultaneously. When the question of Christianity reached Iceland around the year 1000, it arrived not as a royal decree but as a political crisis that threatened to split the island's fragile social unity.

Christian and pagan factions had developed within Icelandic society, and the tension between them was becoming dangerous. The Althing convened to resolve the question, and the task of deciding fell to the lawspeaker — the man responsible for memorizing and reciting Iceland's laws — a pagan chieftain named Þorgeirr Ljósvetningagoði. He retired under his cloak for a day and a night, alone with whatever thoughts occupy a man asked to decide the religious identity of an entire society.

When he emerged, his decision was characteristically Icelandic in its practicality. Iceland would officially become Christian. All public worship of the old gods would cease, all children would be baptized. But the old practices could continue in private. Eating horse meat — prohibited by the church — would remain permitted. Exposure of unwanted infants, though discouraged, would not be criminalized immediately. The conversion was real, but so was the accommodation.

Þorgeirr then went home and threw his carved idols of the Norse gods into a waterfall — a gesture of personal commitment from the man who had just negotiated the most tolerant conversion agreement in Scandinavian history. The waterfall is still called Goðafoss: the waterfall of the gods.

Uppsala: The Last Temple

While Denmark and Norway moved into the Christian era during the tenth and eleventh centuries, Sweden held out longer — and nowhere more stubbornly than at Uppsala, the great religious center of the Swedish interior, where the old gods were worshipped at a scale and elaborateness that had no parallel elsewhere in Scandinavia.

The German cleric Adam of Bremen visited Uppsala around 1070 and left an account that reads, even across a thousand years, with the quality of genuine astonishment. He described a magnificent temple gleaming with gold, surrounded by a sacred grove where trees were never allowed to die.

Inside the temple stood three great idols: Thor in the center, flanked by Odin and Freyr. Every nine years, the people of Sweden gathered for a great sacrificial festival that lasted nine days. Each day, nine males of every living species were offered — humans included, their bodies hung alongside animals in the branches of the sacred trees.

Adam was a Christian writing for a Christian audience, and his account needs to be read with appropriate skepticism — he was not a neutral observer, and the details of human sacrifice may have been exaggerated for rhetorical effect. But the broad outline is confirmed by other sources, and what Uppsala represented is clear enough: a functioning, well-organized religious institution with the resources and the social support to sustain large-scale public ritual well into the period when its Danish and Norwegian equivalents had already been dismantled.

The temple at Uppsala was destroyed sometime around 1090, when the Swedish king Inge the Elder — who had already been driven from his throne once for refusing to perform the traditional sacrifices — finally consolidated enough power to impose Christianity on the holdouts. The sacred grove was cut down. The temple was demolished, and a Christian church was built on the site. The last major center of public Norse Paganism in Scandinavia was gone.

Syncretism in Stone and Metal

The physical objects of the conversion period tell a more nuanced story than the political narrative of kings and temples.

Throughout Scandinavia, the craftsmen and artists of the tenth and eleventh centuries produced work that moved fluidly between the two religious worlds. The Jelling style of Viking art — fluid, interlaced animal forms — was applied equally to Christian and pagan subjects, producing objects where the imagery of the old religion and the new were aesthetically inseparable. Pendants were made that could be read as either a cross or Thor's hammer depending on the angle and the inclination of the viewer. Churches were decorated with carvings of Norse mythological scenes alongside biblical ones — Sigurd killing the dragon on the same stone as Christ the pantocrator.

This was not confusion. It was continuity — an artistic tradition working with new material while remaining true to its own aesthetic logic. The craftsmen who made these objects were not theological relativists. They were people doing what craftsmen always do: serving the tastes of their patrons and the demands of their market, in a period when those tastes and demands were genuinely mixed.

The runestones of the period reflect the same dynamic. Hundreds of runestones from the eleventh century bear Christian formulas — prayers for the soul of the deceased, invocations of God and the saints — carved in the ancient sacred alphabet of the old religion, in forms that are structurally identical to pre-Christian memorial stones. The medium was pagan. The message was Christian. The people who commissioned them apparently saw no contradiction.

The Role of the Kings

The Christianization of Scandinavia was, in the end, largely driven from the top. It was kings, not missionaries, who determined the pace and shape of the transition — and they did so for reasons that had as much to do with political consolidation as with spiritual conviction.

The Viking Age was, in its early centuries, a world without kings in the modern sense. Scandinavia was governed by a shifting landscape of chieftains and warlords, each controlling territory through personal loyalty, military capacity, and the redistribution of wealth. Christianity offered something this system lacked: an ideological framework for centralized royal authority. A Christian king ruled by divine right, answerable to God and to the church, with a legitimacy that transcended the local and the personal. For ambitious rulers trying to consolidate power across large territories, this was not a minor advantage.

The shift from chieftains to kings happened gradually across the Viking Age, and Christianity was part of the mechanism. Rulers who converted gained access to the administrative and literary infrastructure of the church — the ability to produce written documents, maintain records, correspond with other European monarchs on equal terms. They gained political recognition from Christian powers that could provide military support or commercial access. And they gained a new vocabulary for authority that the old religion, with its warrior ethos and its distributed loyalties, had never quite provided.

What Remained

By the end of the eleventh century, Scandinavia was, in the official sense, Christian. Churches had been built on the sites of old pagan temples. The great public sacrificial feasts — the *blóts* that had marked the rhythm of the Norse religious year — had been replaced by the Christian liturgical calendar. The missionaries had won, at least on paper.

What remained was harder to measure and harder to eradicate. The old stories survived, passed down in households and eventually written down by men like Snorri Sturluson, who understood that a mythology is a form of cultural memory and that losing it entirely would be a different kind of impoverishment. The old practices persisted in modified forms: harvest observances, protective rituals, the quiet leaving of offerings in places that had been sacred long before a church was built on top of them.

The names of the Norse gods survived in the days of the week — a legacy so embedded in the Germanic languages that no one notices it anymore. Tuesday is Tyr's day. Wednesday is Woden's day, Woden being the Anglo-Saxon cognate of Odin. Thursday belongs to Thor. Friday to Frigg, or Freya, depending on which scholar you ask.

And the stories themselves — the Eddas, the Sagas, the myths that Sturluson assembled into a coherent account before they could disappear entirely — survived to become the foundation of a literary and spiritual tradition that is still very much alive. The people we will meet later in this book, practicing Asatru in Iceland or holding blóts in American backyards, are inheritors of something that Christianity never quite managed to finish erasing.

The Norse gods, it turns out, are difficult to kill. Even Ragnarök, as we will see, does not quite manage it.

Chapter Five

The Creation of the Cosmos

Every religion begins with the same question. Before the gods, before the world, before anything — what was there?

The Norse answer is one of the strangest and most compelling creation myths in human history. It does not begin with light, or with a divine word, or with a benevolent power deciding to make something out of nothing. It begins with ice and fire, with a void so vast and so silent that the word "emptiness" barely covers it, and with a giant whose body became the world we live in. It is a creation story that feels, even now, genuinely weird — and that weirdness, on reflection, turns out to be part of its honesty. The universe the Norse imagined was not built for human comfort. It was built from violence and accident and the repurposing of something enormous that had no say in the matter.

Understanding this myth is not optional context for Norse Paganism. It is the foundation on which everything else rests. The gods, the nine worlds, Yggdrasil, the Norns, Ragnarök — none of it makes complete sense without knowing where it all came from and, crucially, what it was made of.

Ginnungagap: The Void Before Everything

In the beginning, there was Ginnungagap.

The word is Old Norse, and it resists clean translation. *Ginnunga* carries connotations of magic, of illusion, of something charged with latent power. *Gap* is simply gap — an opening, an absence, a space between things. Ginnungagap is the primordial void: not nothing, exactly, but a vast, dark, silent emptiness that existed before anything else did, and within which everything else would eventually form.

On one side of Ginnungagap lay Niflheim — a world of mist, ice, and bitter cold, from which eleven rivers flowed outward into the void. These rivers are collectively known as the Élivágar, and as they traveled away from their source, they froze, depositing layers of ice and rime into the emptiness. On the opposite side lay Muspelheim — a world of fire and heat, roaring with flame, its sparks and embers drifting across the void toward the ice.

Where the cold and the heat met in the middle of Ginnungagap, something happened. The ice began to melt. The meltwater gathered, animated by the warmth, and from it emerged the first being: a giant named Ymir.

Ymir and the First Life

Ymir was not created by anyone. He simply condensed out of the interaction between ice and fire, the way frost forms on a cold surface or steam rises from hot water — a natural consequence of two opposing forces meeting in the right conditions. He was the first living thing, and he was enormous, and he was not alone for long.

As Ymir slept, he sweated, and from his sweat came the first other beings: a man and a woman who emerged from beneath his left arm, and a six-headed giant who grew from his legs. These were the first of the frost giants — the *jötnar* — who would become, in Norse mythology, the ancient adversaries of the gods, the forces of chaos and wildness that the divine order was always struggling to contain.

Alongside Ymir, the melting ice also produced a cow named Auðumbla — four rivers of milk flowed from her udder, providing Ymir with sustenance. Auðumbla fed herself by licking the salty ice blocks of Ginnungagap, and as she licked, she slowly revealed another figure buried within the ice: a being named Búri, the first of a different kind — the ancestor of the gods.

Búri had a son named Borr. Borr married a giantess named Bestla, and together they had three sons: Odin, Vili, and Vé. The gods had arrived — and they were, from the very beginning, half giant on their mother's side. The divine and the monstrous were never entirely separate categories in Norse cosmology. They were family.

The Killing of Ymir

The three brothers — Odin, Vili, and Vé — killed Ymir.

The sources do not dwell on their motivation. Ymir was the first being, the origin of the frost giants, and perhaps simply too much of a problem to leave alive. What the sources do dwell on, in considerable detail, is what the brothers did with the body.

They dragged Ymir's corpse to the center of Ginnungagap and built the world from it.

His flesh became the earth. His blood became the seas and lakes — so much blood that all the frost giants drowned in the flood of it, except for one, named Bergelmir, who survived with his family by climbing onto a boat and waiting for the waters to recede. His bones became the mountains. His teeth and fragments of his shattered bones became the rocks and stones scattered across the landscape. His hair became the trees. His skull became the dome of the sky, held up at its four corners by four dwarves named Norðri, Suðri, Austri, and Vestri — North, South, East, and West. The sparks and embers that flew from Muspelheim were set in the sky to become the stars.

Then the brothers shaped the earth itself into regions. The land at the center, encircled by a great ocean, they called Midgard — Middle Enclosure — and reserved it for a new kind of being they intended to create. The outer regions, wild and inhospitable, they left for the giants.

It is worth sitting with the strangeness of this for a moment. The world in Norse cosmology is not a created place in the sense that most traditions use the word. It is a repurposed corpse. The ground beneath your feet is the flesh of a dead giant. The sky above you is his skull. The oceans are his blood. This is not a universe designed for human habitation by a benevolent deity. It is a universe improvised from available materials by three brothers who needed somewhere to put things.

The First Humans

The world had been built, but it was empty. Odin, Vili, and Vé walked across the new earth and found two trees — an ash and an elm — lying on the ground. Some sources describe them as barely alive, without breath or warmth or color. The three brothers stopped and gave them gifts.

Odin gave them breath and life. Vili gave them intelligence and the ability to move. Vé gave them the capacity to speak, to see, and to hear. The ash tree became the first man, named Askr. The elm became the first woman, named Embla. Together they were given Midgard as their home, and from them descended the whole of humanity.

The Norse creation of humanity is striking in its intimacy. There is no clay, no divine breath into a formed body, no rib taken from a sleeping man. There are two trees, found by chance during a walk, transformed by three brothers who apparently decided, in the moment, to make people. The arbitrariness of it — the sense that humans exist not because we were planned but because we happened to be in the right place when the gods were passing through — gives the Norse creation story a texture that feels very different from traditions in which humanity is the central purpose of the whole enterprise.

Yggdrasil: The Tree That Holds Everything Together

At the center of the newly created cosmos stands Yggdrasil — the World Tree, an ash of incomprehensible size whose branches reach into the heavens and whose three roots extend into three different realms: one into Asgard, the home of the gods; one into Jotunheim, the realm of the giants; and one into Niflheim, the cold world of the dead.

Yggdrasil is not merely a large tree. It is the structural spine of the cosmos — the thing that connects the nine worlds and holds them in relation to each other. Its health is the health of everything. When, at the approach of Ragnarök, Yggdrasil begins to shake and groan, it is not just a dramatic special effect. It is a sign that the fabric holding the universe together is failing.

The tree is home to a remarkable collection of inhabitants. An eagle of immense wisdom sits in its highest branches, and between its eyes perches a hawk named Veðrfölnir. At its roots in Niflheim, the dragon Níðhöggr gnaws perpetually at the wood — a slow, patient destruction that has been going on since the tree first grew and will presumably continue until Ragnarök makes it irrelevant. Running up and down the trunk between the eagle and the dragon goes a squirrel named Ratatoskr, carrying insults and provocations from one to the other, stirring conflict for reasons that are never entirely explained but feel entirely plausible. Four stags — Dáinn, Dvalinn, Duneyrr, and Duraþrór — wander among the branches, nibbling at the foliage, while a goat named Heiðrún feeds on the leaves of the tree and produces, from her udder, the endless mead that the warriors of Valhalla drink each night.

Beneath one of Yggdrasil's roots lies the well of Urðarbrunnr — the Well of Urðr, or the Well of Fate — and it is here that the gods hold their daily council, riding the rainbow bridge Bifrost to assemble beneath the branches of the World Tree. The well is tended by three figures who are among the most important in all of Norse mythology, and who are also among the least discussed.

The Norns: Weavers of Fate

At the Well of Urðr sit the Norns — three women named Urðr, Verðandi, and Skuld, whose names translate roughly as What Has Been, What Is Becoming, and What Shall Be. They weave the threads of fate for every living being: gods, humans, giants, and creatures of every kind. What they weave cannot be unwoven. What they decree cannot be appealed.

The Norns are not goddesses in the conventional sense — they do not belong to either the Aesir or the Vanir tribes, and they are not worshipped in the way that Odin or Thor or Freya are worshipped. They are something older and more fundamental than the gods: the mechanism by which destiny operates, the force that even Odin cannot override, however hard he tries.

And Odin does try. Much of what he does — the sacrifices he makes, the knowledge he pursues, the ravens he sends out to gather information, the seeresses he consults and the dead he raises to question — is an attempt to see past the veil that the Norns control, to know what is coming and perhaps find some way to prepare for it or delay it. He never quite succeeds. The Norns continue their weaving regardless.

The three Norns also tend to Yggdrasil itself, drawing water from the Well of Urðr and mixing it with the white clay that surrounds it to pour over the tree's roots, keeping it alive. The World Tree's health depends on the attention of the very beings who determine the fate of everything the tree sustains. The cosmological logic is circular in a way that feels deliberate: fate maintains the structure that fate operates within.

Other Norns appear in the sources beyond these three — lesser figures who attend individual humans at birth and weave their personal destinies. Some bring good fortune, others bad, and the difference appears to depend less on the merit of the person being born than on which Norns happen to show up. This is a cosmology in which luck is real and not entirely random, in which the circumstances of your birth shape what is possible for you in ways that no amount of effort can entirely overcome. It is a view of the world that would have felt intuitively true to people living in a society where the family you were born into determined almost everything about your life.

A Cosmos Built for What Comes Next

What is perhaps most remarkable about the Norse creation myth is that it contains, from the very beginning, the seeds of its own ending.

Níðhöggr is already chewing at the roots of Yggdrasil. The frost giants — descendants of Bergelmir, who survived the flood of Ymir's blood — are already out there in Jotunheim, nursing the memory of what Odin and his brothers did to their ancestor. The Norns are already weaving fates that the gods cannot see clearly and cannot change. Ragnarök is not a surprise that arrives from outside the system. It is built into the system from the moment of creation, the inevitable consequence of a world made from violence and maintained by forces that the gods do not fully control.

This is what makes Norse cosmology feel so different from creation myths in which the world is fundamentally good, fundamentally purposeful, and fundamentally oriented toward some positive destination. The Norse universe is magnificent, intricate, and populated with extraordinary beings — but it is not safe, and it was never meant to be permanent. It is a temporary arrangement, improvised from a dead giant's body, held together by a tree that something is always gnawing at.

For the people who believed this, it was not a cause for despair. It was a framework for courage. If the world was always going to end, and if even the gods were going to die when it did, then the question was not how to prevent that ending but how to live well within the time available. How to be generous, honorable, and brave. How to make a name that would be remembered after you were gone.

That question — and the various answers Norse Paganism offered to it — is what the rest of this book is about.

CHAPTER SIX

Runes and Magic

There is a moment, somewhere in the process of learning about Norse Paganism, when you realize that the word "magic" requires renegotiation.

In the modern world, magic is a category of things that do not work. It is the rabbit from the hat, the card forced on a willing audience, the illusion sustained by misdirection and the audience's desire to be fooled. When we call something magical we usually mean it is either entertaining or delusional, and we have known for long enough which is which that the distinction barely needs stating. The supernatural has been cordoned off from the natural. The boundary is policed by physics, and physics has not lost a case in several centuries.

The Norse Pagans did not live on this side of that boundary. For them, the world was not divided into the natural and the supernatural — it was a single continuous reality in which certain people, certain objects, and certain practices had access to forces that others did not. Magic was not a departure from how the world worked. It was a deeper engagement with how the world worked. Understanding this is not optional for understanding Norse Paganism. It is the whole point.

A World Full of Spirits

The foundation of Norse magical thinking was animism — the same belief we encountered in the first chapter among the Sami people, and not coincidentally so. The pre-Christian Germanic world held that spirit was not confined to humans or to the gods. Animals had it. Trees had it. Rivers, rocks, and winds had it. A Viking's ship had a spirit — which is why ships were given names, treated with respect, and sometimes launched with blood. A sword of particular quality had a spirit — which is why great swords in the sagas have names and histories and occasionally opinions about who should wield them.

This was not metaphor. It was cosmology. If everything in the world has a consciousness and a will of its own, then everything in the world is also a potential ally or adversary, and the person who knows how to negotiate with those wills has access to power that the ignorant do not. Magic, in this framework, is essentially skilled diplomacy with the non-human world.

The practitioners who were most skilled at this diplomacy were women. This is a consistent pattern in the sources, and it is worth being direct about: in Norse society, magic was gendered female. Men who practiced it risked a social stigma so severe that it had its own word — *ergi* — connoting unmanliness, a transgression of the gender order serious enough to be grounds for legal action. Even Odin, the most magically powerful of all the gods and an enthusiastic practitioner of the highest forms of Norse magic, was mocked for it. The king of the gods doing women's work was, by the standards of Viking Age Scandinavia, at least a little embarrassing.

The women who practiced magic were not, in the Norse conception, doing anything shameful. They were doing something necessary, powerful, and set apart — which is a different thing entirely.

Seiðr: The Magic of Fate

The most significant form of magic in the Norse world was *seiðr* — a practice so central to the religion that understanding it is essential to understanding the völva, the Norns, the goddess Freya, and much of what Odin does when he is not fighting giants or collecting dead warriors.

Seiðr was, at its core, a magic of fate. Its practitioners could perceive the threads of destiny that the Norns were weaving — see the likely futures of individuals, communities, weather systems, military campaigns. More remarkably, they could intervene in those threads: strengthen a favorable fate, weaken an unfavorable one, redirect the course of events through techniques that the sources describe in terms of weaving and spinning. The metaphor is not accidental. Fate in Norse cosmology was literally woven, and seiðr was the skill of working with the material.

The archaeologist Neil Price has spent considerable time reconstructing what seiðr practice actually looked like, drawing on the saga accounts and the material evidence of excavated sites. His summary of the practice's capabilities is worth quoting in full, because it gives a sense of how comprehensive the Norse conception of magical power was:

"There were senior rituals for divination and clairvoyance; for seeking out the hidden, both in the secrets of the mind and in physical locations; for healing the sick; for bringing good luck; for controlling the weather; for calling game animals and fish. Importantly, it could also be used for the opposite of these things — to curse an individual or an enterprise; to blight the land and make it barren; to induce illness; to tell false futures and thus set their recipients on the road to disaster; to injure, maim, and kill."

There was, in other words, no inherent moral direction to seiðr. It was a tool, and what it did depended on who was using it and why. The Norse moral framework around magic was not about the magic itself but about the intentions and the social context of its use. A völva who used seiðr to ensure a good harvest was a community asset. The same völva using the same techniques to blight a neighbor's crops was a dangerous enemy.

The Völva

The professional practitioners of seiðr were called *völur* — singular *völva* — and they were among the most distinctive figures in Norse society.

A völva traveled. This was fundamental to the role — she was not attached to a single community but moved between them, arriving when summoned, performing her rituals for whatever household or settlement needed her services, and moving on. The saga accounts describe her arrival as an event: the household would prepare a special high seat for her, cook particular foods that she ate alone before the ritual, and gather the community to participate in the ceremony that followed.

The ritual itself centered on a form of trance induced through a specific kind of chanting called *varðlokur* — songs whose purpose was to call the spirits that would assist the völva in her journey through other realms. She would sit on her high seat, staff in hand, and as the singing rose around her, she would enter the altered state in which her deeper sight became available. The staff was not decorative. It was a tool and a marker of identity — the material object that defined the völva's role as surely as a sword defined a warrior's.

We know something about what these women looked like from the grave finds. In 1894, a burial was excavated at Köpingsvik on the Swedish island of Öland that has become one of the most studied völva graves on record. The woman buried there was accompanied by a staff of iron, a pouch containing seeds of the psychoactive plant henbane, and a collection of small objects that Price and other researchers have identified as tools of magical practice. A similar grave found at Fyrkat in Denmark, dating to around the tenth century, contained the body of a woman buried in a wagon — itself a statement of status and movement — dressed in an elaborate blue and red garment with white sleeves, wearing silver toe rings of a type found nowhere else in Denmark, and accompanied by her seiðr staff.

The henbane is significant. The plant produces powerful hallucinogenic effects when absorbed through the skin or consumed in small quantities, and its presence in multiple völva graves suggests that the altered states the practitioners entered were chemically assisted — not faked, not performed, but genuinely experienced. This changes how we understand the claims the sagas make about what völur could perceive and do. These were not women pretending to see things. They were women who, in a very real neurological sense, were seeing things — things whose interpretation was shaped by the cosmological framework they inhabited and the expectations of the community watching them.

The völva's life expectancy was not, the evidence suggests, particularly long. Repeated exposure to hallucinogenic plants takes a toll. Several saga accounts mention that the practice shortened the practitioner's life, and there is something in the archaeological record that supports this — the care with which völur were buried, their graves rich with objects and attention, suggests that communities understood themselves to be losing something valuable when these women died.

Galdr: The Magic of Sound

Alongside seiðr, the Norse practiced a different form of magic called *galdr* — a word derived from the Old Norse verb meaning to crow or to sing, which gives some indication of what it involved.

Where seiðr was primarily divinatory and fate-working, galdr was incantatory — the use of specific sung or chanted verses to produce specific effects in the world. The *galdrar* were not improvised. They were formulas, precise sequences of words and sounds whose power derived from their correct performance, much as a chemical reaction requires the right substances in the right proportions. Change the formula and you change — or destroy — the effect.

The saga literature preserves accounts of galdr being used for a remarkable range of purposes: raising the dead to question them, calming storms at sea, healing wounds, blunting enemy weapons, cursing opponents, protecting ships and their crews, easing difficult childbirth. The list in the *Hávamál* — the Old Norse poem attributed to Odin himself — includes eighteen distinct magical songs, each with its own specific application, from waking the hanged to turning an enemy's weapons against him.

Galdr intersected with runic knowledge in ways that are not always easy to separate clearly. Many of the most powerful galdrar were said to involve the speaking or singing of runic formulas — the letters themselves acting as concentrations of cosmological power that the human voice could activate. This brings us to the runes.

The Runes

Few things in Norse culture are more consistently misunderstood than runes. In popular culture they have become a kind of generic mystical shorthand — ancient symbols drawn on stones and cards, available for purchase in gift shops, used for everything from divination to interior decoration. This trivialization does them a disservice, because the actual history and function of runes is considerably more interesting than their gift-shop afterlife suggests.

Runes were, first and most practically, an alphabet. The Elder Futhark — named for its first six letters, Fehu, Uruz, Thurisaz, Ansuz, Raidho, and Kaunan — consisted of twenty-four characters used by the Germanic and Norse peoples from roughly the first century C.E. onward to write inscriptions on objects, stones, and occasionally organic materials like wood and bone. They were later supplemented by the Younger Futhark, a sixteen-character alphabet that became standard across Scandinavia during the Viking Age, and by the Anglo-Saxon Futhorc, a variant used in England that expanded to thirty-three characters.

The name *rune* itself — in Old Norse *rún* — means secret, mystery, or whispered counsel. This is not a coincidence. From the beginning, the runic letters were understood to be more than mere notation. Each rune was an individual symbol that represented, simultaneously, a sound, a name, and a cosmological principle — a concentration of meaning that went far beyond the phonetic value the letter carried in ordinary writing.

The Meaning of Each Rune

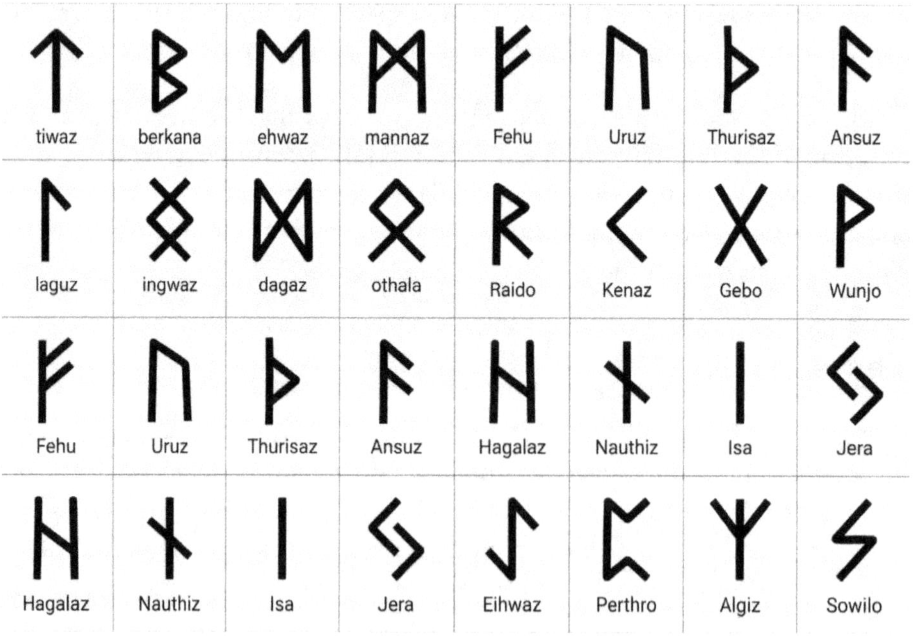

ᛏ tiwaz	ᛒ berkana	ᛖ ehwaz	ᛗ mannaz	ᚠ Fehu	ᚢ Uruz	ᚦ Thurisaz	ᚨ Ansuz
ᛚ laguz	ᛝ ingwaz	ᛞ dagaz	ᛟ othala	ᚱ Raido	ᚲ Kenaz	ᚷ Gebo	ᚹ Wunjo
ᚠ Fehu	ᚢ Uruz	ᚦ Thurisaz	ᚨ Ansuz	ᚺ Hagalaz	ᚾ Nauthiz	ᛁ Isa	ᛃ Jera
ᚺ Hagalaz	ᚾ Nauthiz	ᛁ Isa	ᛃ Jera	ᛇ Eihwaz	ᛈ Perthro	ᛉ Algiz	ᛊ Sowilo

Understanding what the runes actually meant to the people who used them requires knowing what each one carried. What follows is not an exhaustive account — scholars have filled entire volumes with the interpretation of individual runes — but a working introduction to the twenty-four letters of the Elder Futhark and the principles they embodied.

Fehu — cattle, wealth, abundance. The rune of material prosperity and the responsibilities that come with it. In a society where cattle were the primary measure of wealth, fehu carried the weight of everything that ownership meant: security, status, obligation to kin.

Uruz — the aurochs, the wild ox. Raw strength, untamed vitality, the power of the natural world before it is domesticated. Where fehu represents wealth managed and distributed, uruz represents the force that has not yet been brought under control.

Thurisaz — the giant, the thorn. A rune of directed force and conflict, associated with the frost giants and with Thor's power against them. It carries both danger and protection, depending on how it is used and against whom.

Ansuz — the god, specifically Odin. The rune of divine communication, of speech, poetry, and the kind of wisdom that arrives as inspiration rather than as the product of deliberate reasoning. It is the rune of the mouth and the mind working together.

Raidho — the ride, the journey. Movement through the world, but also the ordered movement of the cosmos — the sun's daily path, the rhythm of the seasons. A rune of righteous travel and the proper conduct of a journey.

Kaunan — the torch, or in some readings, ulcer or wound. A rune of controlled fire, of the light that humans make against the dark, but also of the pain that burns from within. It represents both the gift of fire and the cost of that gift.

Gebo — the gift. One of the most socially significant runes, because in Norse culture the gift was never simple. Every gift created an obligation, a relationship, a bond between giver and receiver. Gebo encodes the entire Norse economy of generosity and reciprocity.

Wunjo — joy, harmony, the clan in good order. The rune of the well-functioning community, of people working together in their proper roles, of the pleasure that comes when things are as they should be.

Hagalaz — hail. The destructive power of nature, sudden and indiscriminate, transforming the landscape without warning. A rune of disruption and the forces that cannot be predicted or controlled, only endured.

Nauthiz — need, necessity, constraint. The rune of hardship endured, of the friction between what is and what is needed. It carries within it the idea that necessity is also a teacher — that the things we are forced to do without shape us in ways that abundance cannot.

Isa — ice. Stillness, stasis, the freezing of movement and change. Not always negative — sometimes what is needed is for things to stop moving long enough to be seen clearly — but always a rune of pause and of forces suspended rather than resolved.

Jera — the year, the harvest, the reward of patient labor. The rune of cycles and of natural justice — the idea that what is planted in good faith, tended carefully, will eventually yield what was promised. Time moves, and the harvest comes.

Eihwaz — the yew tree. One of the most complex runes, associated simultaneously with life and death — the yew is both poisonous and extraordinarily long-lived, its wood used for bows and its presence marking sacred and burial sites. Eihwaz points toward Yggdrasil and the axis connecting the worlds.

Perthro — fate, the unknown, the lot cast in darkness. Often associated with a dice cup or a well, perthro represents the element of chance within the weaving of fate — the things that even the Norns hold in suspension until the moment of their revelation.

Algiz — protection, the outstretched hand, the elk's antlers. A rune of defense and of the connection between the human and the divine — the reaching upward toward the gods and the shelter that reaching provides.

Sowilo — the sun. Victory, vitality, the force that drives away darkness. In a northern climate where the sun's return after winter was a genuine relief rather than a given, sowilo carried emotional weight that is hard to fully appreciate from a temperate perspective.

Tiwaz — the god Tyr, justice, sacrifice for the greater good. The rune of the thing — the legal assembly — and of the willingness to give something up so that the community can function. Tyr lost his hand binding Fenrir, and the rune carries that cost.

Berkano — the birch tree, birth, new beginnings. A rune of growth, of the feminine forces of nurturing and renewal, of the spring returning after winter. Associated with female mysteries and the cycles of the body.

Ehwaz — the horse, partnership, trust between two beings working together. The relationship between a rider and a horse was one of the most intimate and consequential bonds in Norse life, and this rune encodes the mutuality that made it work.

Mannaz — the human being, the self in relation to the community. The rune of what it means to be a person — not in isolation but embedded in a web of relationships, obligations, and shared identity.

Laguz — water, the sea, the unconscious, the flow of things that cannot be contained. The rune of the Norse relationship with the ocean — both the trade route and the grave, the source of wealth and the source of terror.

Ingwaz — the god Freyr, fertility, the stored potential of the seed before it sprouts. A rune of completion and of the gestation period between action and result — the harvest that has not yet arrived but is already determined.

Dagaz — the day, the dawn, the transformative moment between darkness and light. A rune of breakthrough and of the change that comes suddenly, at the threshold between one state and another.

Othala — the ancestral estate, the inherited homeland, the bonds of blood and place. The rune of what is passed down through generations — not just land and property but identity, memory, and the obligations that come with belonging to a lineage.

Runes in Practice

The runic alphabet was used in practice across an enormous range of contexts, from the mundane to the deeply sacred. Runestones — standing stones carved with commemorative or dedicatory inscriptions — are the most visible surviving evidence of runic culture, and Scandinavia still has thousands of them. The earliest confirmed runic inscription is found on a comb of antler from Denmark, dating to around 150 C.E., bearing only a single word: *harja*, a man's name. Someone labeled their comb. The technology of writing arrived in Scandinavia and immediately found its first application in personal property marking, which is either touching or very human depending on your perspective.

The saga literature preserves accounts of runes used for healing, cursing, protection in battle, and communication across distances. The story of Egil's Saga — in which the hero Egil discovers that a sick girl's illness has been caused by incorrectly carved runes placed under her bed, destroys them, and replaces them with correctly carved ones that cure her — is the most famous of these accounts, and it illustrates several things simultaneously: that runic knowledge was considered genuinely powerful, that incorrect use of that power was genuinely dangerous, and that the power was accessible to those who had the knowledge, not confined to a priestly class.

What the story also shows, and what the saga tradition generally confirms, is that runic literacy was not universal but was not esoteric either. Knowing how to carve runes was a skill, like knowing how to forge iron or navigate by stars — something not everyone had but something that ordinary people could and did acquire. The person who carved protective runes on a ship's keel or a house's threshold was not performing a priestly function. They were doing practical work with practical tools, using the cosmological forces encoded in the letters to do something useful.

The runes carved on weapons and personal objects communicated this same practicality. An axe with a runic inscription was not merely a labeled axe. It was an axe whose purpose had been declared to the forces encoded in the letters — a tool whose function had been aligned with a cosmological principle. The line between craftsmanship and magic, in this context, was not clear because it was not thought to exist.

The Legacy in Stone

The runestones that dot the Scandinavian landscape — more than six thousand survive in Sweden alone — are the most durable record of a culture that was in many ways oral rather than written. They commemorate the dead, mark boundaries, record journeys and achievements, offer warnings and protections, and occasionally say things that resist all interpretation even after centuries of scholarly attention.

Many of them are explicitly Christian — erected after the conversion, invoking God and Christ alongside the runic script. This combination, which might seem contradictory, was perfectly natural to the people who commissioned them. The runes were a technology, not a religion. They could be used to write anything.

What they leave behind is the sense of a world in which writing and power were not yet fully separated — in which the act of carving a word was understood to do something to the reality that word named. That understanding did not survive the conversion intact. But its traces are still visible in the stones, patient and permanent, waiting for anyone who takes the time to read them.

Chapter Seven

The Nine Worlds

The Norse cosmos is not a single place. It is nine places, stacked and branching along the limbs of Yggdrasil like rooms in an impossibly large house — some bright and ordered, some wild and dangerous, some so cold or so dark that the sources barely describe them at all, as if the imagination falters at the threshold.

We have already met Yggdrasil in Chapter 5, the World Tree whose roots anchor the cosmos and whose branches hold the nine worlds in relation to each other. What we have not yet done is walk through those worlds individually — to look at what each one contains, who lives there, what the rules are, and why any of it matters to the Norse people who imagined it. That is the work of this chapter.

It is worth noting, before we begin, that the Norse sources are not always consistent about the nine worlds. Different poems in the Poetic Edda, different sections of the Prose Edda, and different saga accounts emphasize different details, occasionally contradict each other, and leave large areas simply unaddressed. There was never an authoritative Norse cosmological map — no official document that laid out the geography of the nine worlds with the precision of a modern atlas. What we have instead is an accumulation of references, images, and narrative fragments from which scholars have reconstructed a picture that is coherent enough to work with but should not be mistaken for completeness.

With that caveat in place, let us begin at the center and work outward.

Midgard: The World of Humans

Midgard is where we live. The name translates from Old Norse as Middle Enclosure — the inhabited world, set at the center of the cosmic structure, surrounded by the ocean and by the territories of beings considerably more powerful than its human occupants.

It was made, as we saw in the previous chapter, from the flesh of Ymir, shaped by Odin and his brothers into land and sea and sky. It was given to humanity — to Askr and Embla, the first man and woman made from ash and elm — as their domain, and it is protected from the giants of the outer realms by a great wall built by the gods from Ymir's eyebrows. This detail, which sounds faintly absurd in isolation, carries a cosmological logic: the boundary between the human world and the wild world beyond it is made of the same substance as the world itself — a repurposing of the monstrous to serve the ordered.

Midgard is connected to Asgard above it by the Bifrost — the rainbow bridge whose colors, in Norse understanding, were the visible sign of the fire through which it burned. Only the gods could travel Bifrost freely. Humans who tried to cross it would be consumed by the heat. The connection between the human world and the divine one was real and visible, arching across the sky every time it rained — but it was not a crossing that mortals were invited to make under their own power.

Midgard sits above the realm of the dead and below the realm of the gods. Its position is neither the highest nor the lowest, and this is cosmologically honest — humans in Norse belief occupied a middle rank in the order of things, not the pinnacle of creation but not insignificant either. The gods cared about what happened in Midgard. They watched it, visited it, interfered in it, and would ultimately die defending it.

Beneath the surface of Midgard's encircling ocean lives the Midgard Serpent — Jörmungandr, child of Loki and the giantess Angrboða, cast into the sea by Odin who recognized the danger it represented. Jörmungandr grew until it encircled the entire world, its tail in its own mouth — which is why it is sometimes called the Ouroboros, though that name comes from a different tradition. It is one of Loki's three terrible children, and its role in Ragnarök —

its battle with Thor that kills them both — is already written into the cosmos from the moment it is thrown into the sea.

Asgard: The Home of the Gods

Asgard is the highest of the nine worlds, situated at the top of Yggdrasil, home to the Aesir tribe of gods and the site of everything most magnificent in Norse cosmology.

It is an ordered place — a realm of law, hierarchy, and deliberate structure. The gods hold their council here daily, riding across Bifrost to assemble at the Well of Urðr beneath the World Tree. The halls of Asgard are described in the sources with the kind of detail that suggests genuine imaginative investment: roofs of silver and gold, walls built from precious materials, spaces large enough to house the armies of the dead that will fight at Ragnarök.

The most famous of Asgard's structures is Valhalla — the Hall of the Slain, where Odin receives the warriors chosen for him by the Valkyries, who feast and fight and wait for the end of the world. We will meet Valhalla properly in the chapter on death and the afterlife. For now, it is enough to note that it is the most famous room in the most famous building in the most powerful realm in the Norse cosmos, and that it is essentially a barracks for dead soldiers that happens to have very good catering.

Alongside Valhalla stands Glaðsheimr — the bright home, where Odin's throne Hliðskjálf is located. From this throne, Odin can see everything that happens across all nine worlds. It is both a statement of his authority and an explanation of his character: a god who can see everything, knows that he cannot stop what is coming, and watches anyway. Also in Asgard is Fólkvangr — the Field of the People, where Freya receives her half of the battle-slain — and Himinbjörg, where Heimdall stands his endless watch at the edge of Bifrost, listening for threats.

Asgard was not always as secure as it appeared. The wall surrounding it was built by a giant who negotiated a contract with the gods — Freya, the sun, and the moon in exchange for completing the wall in a single winter. The gods agreed, assuming it was impossible, and were horrified when the giant and his horse Svaðilfari began making rapid progress. Loki, responsible for talking the gods into the contract in the first place, was sent to sabotage it, which he did by transforming into a mare and distracting Svaðilfari. The wall was not finished in time, the giant received nothing, and Thor killed him when he became violent about it. Loki, in his mare form, subsequently gave birth to an eight-legged horse named Sleipnir, who became Odin's preferred mount. This is the kind of story that Norse mythology produces regularly — cosmological consequence generated by a sequence of decisions that seemed reasonable at each individual step and catastrophic in combination.

Vanaheim: The Home of the Vanir

Vanaheim is the least described of the nine worlds, which is frustrating given that its inhabitants — the Vanir gods — are among the most important in the Norse pantheon.

The Vanir are the other tribe of gods, distinct from the Aesir in their associations and their character. Where the Aesir are oriented toward war, law, and the masculine virtues of the warrior culture, the Vanir are associated with fertility, nature, magic, and the more fluid forces of growth and abundance. Their principal deities — Freya, Freyr, and Njord — are among the most widely worshipped in the Norse world, and their influence on the religion is enormous.

What Vanaheim itself looks like, the sources largely decline to say. We know it exists, that it is the original home of the Vanir tribe, and that after the war between the Aesir and Vanir that we will discuss in the chapter on the gods, certain deities moved between the two worlds as hostages and ambassadors. The Prose Edda describes it as the place where the god Njord was raised, which tells us almost nothing about its geography or character.

What we can infer from the nature of the Vanir themselves is suggestive. If Asgard is a realm of halls and councils and hierarchical order, Vanaheim may be imagined as something wilder and more fertile — a place where the forces of growth and magic operate without the structuring influence of Odin's law-giving temperament. This is speculation built on inference, which is often the best the sources allow.

Jotunheim: The Realm of the Giants

Jotunheim is the homeland of the giants — the *jötnar* — and it surrounds Midgard in the way that wilderness surrounds a settlement, always present at the edges, always threatening to reclaim what has been carved out of it.

The giants are not, in Norse cosmology, straightforwardly evil. They are ancient — older than the gods, descended from Ymir, the original being from whose body the world was made. They represent the forces of chaos, wildness, and the untamed natural world, which in the Norse understanding were not simply bad things but necessary ones. The cosmos required both order and chaos, both the structured world of Asgard and the wild world of Jotunheim, and the tension between them was not a problem to be solved but the condition under which everything operated.

That said, many of the giants are actively hostile to the gods, and the gods spend considerable effort keeping them out of Asgard and Midgard. Thor makes regular expeditions to Jotunheim specifically to kill giants, which he describes as one of his favorite pastimes, and which the giants presumably regard rather differently. The animosity is not universal — the gods have ongoing relationships with giants that include marriage, trade, and alliance. Odin's mother was a giantess. Thor's mother was a giantess. Freyr married a giantess named Gerðr after falling so completely in love with her that he gave away his sword — the sword he will need at Ragnarök — as a bride price.

The landscape of Jotunheim as the sources describe it is inhospitable: rocky, forested, covered in snow and ice, dominated by a stronghold called Útgarðr — the outer enclosure, as opposed to Midgard's middle enclosure and Asgard's heaven. Útgarðr is ruled by a giant king called Útgarða-Loki — not the same as the trickster god Loki, though the name confusion has produced its share of interpretive headaches. It is a place of illusion and misdirection, where things are not what they appear, and where the gods who venture there often find themselves humiliated before they find their way back.

The giants will be the gods' final opponents at Ragnarök, arriving in their ships and their armies to end the world. They have been waiting for this since the flood of Ymir's blood — patient, ancient, and aware of their place in the cosmic plan.

Muspelheim: The World of Fire

At the opposite extreme from Niflheim — and indeed from almost everywhere else in the cosmos — lies Muspelheim, the primordial realm of fire and heat that existed before the world was made, whose sparks and embers drifting across Ginnungagap were one half of the creative collision that produced Ymir.

Muspelheim is not a place the sources spend much time describing, because there is not much to say about it beyond the fact that it is enormously, lethally hot, full of fire and flame, and inhabited by fire giants and demons whose entire existence is oriented toward the destruction of everything else. Its ruler is Surtr — a fire giant of terrifying power, carrying a flaming sword, who will lead the forces of Muspelheim against the gods at Ragnarök and burn the world to nothing when the battle is done.

Surtr is mentioned in *Völuspá* with the kind of spare, ominous brevity that the poem uses for its most powerful images: he comes from the south with fire, the gods fall, the sun goes dark, the earth sinks into the sea. He is not a character in the way that Odin or Thor or Loki are characters — he has no stories, no personality, no relationships with the other inhabitants of the cosmos. He is a force, present from the beginning, waiting.

The name Muspelheim contains within it the concept of destruction by fire — the world's end anticipated in the world's first element. The Norse cosmos was made partly from fire, and it will be ended by fire, and the symmetry feels intentional.

Alfheim: The World of the Elves

Alfheim is described in the sources as the home of the light elves — beings of luminous, almost divine beauty, associated with fertility and the benevolent forces of nature. The god Freyr was given Alfheim as a gift when he cut his first tooth, which tells us that it was considered a realm of considerable value and that Freyr's connection to its inhabitants was deep and longstanding.

The elves of Norse mythology are not the elves of modern fantasy — not small, not comic, not shoemakers. The *ljósálfar*, the light elves, are described in the Prose Edda as fairer than the sun to look upon — beings of such radiance that the comparison with sunlight felt natural rather than hyperbolic. Their relationship with humans was active and consequential: they could bring illness or health, good fortune or bad, and the minor sacrifices made to the elves — the *álfablót*, a private, household ritual that Christian writers found particularly difficult to stamp out — were a regular feature of Norse religious life.

The Norse sources also mention *dökkálfar* — dark elves — though the distinction between dark elves and dwarves is unclear and possibly not original. Snorri Sturluson attempts to systematize it in the Prose Edda but may be imposing categories that the older tradition did not maintain. What is clear is that the elves occupied a middle position in the cosmic hierarchy — more powerful than humans, less powerful than gods, connected to the natural world in ways that made them worth keeping on good terms.

Nidavellir: The World of the Dwarves

Beneath the ground, in the deep places of the cosmos, live the dwarves — and they are nothing like what popular culture has made of them.

The dwarves of Norse mythology are master craftsmen, the finest makers in all the nine worlds, whose skill at working metal, stone, and wood exceeded that of gods and humans alike. The greatest treasures of the Norse cosmos came from their forges: Thor's hammer Mjölnir, which could destroy any enemy and always returned to its thrower's hand. Odin's spear Gungnir, which never missed its mark. The ring Draupnir, which dripped eight identical rings of equal weight every ninth night. The ship Skiðblaðnir, which could sail any sea and any wind and yet fold up small enough to fit in a pocket. The golden hair of Sif, made to replace the original that Loki cut off as a prank.

The relationship between the gods and the dwarves was ongoing and occasionally tense. The gods needed what the dwarves could make, and the dwarves knew it — they drove hard bargains, and the saga of how Loki commissioned the treasures of the gods from competing dwarf workshops, bet his own head in the process, and then escaped the consequences through a technicality that any lawyer would admire, is one of the funniest and most revealing stories in the tradition.

Dwarves lived underground, worked by firelight, and avoided the sun — which, if it touched them, turned them to stone. This detail is not merely picturesque. It encodes a cosmological logic: the dwarves are beings of the deep earth, of darkness and mineral power, and the sun belongs to a different order of reality that they cannot survive. They were said to have originally been maggots in Ymir's flesh before the gods gave them intelligence and form, which is either a very unglamorous origin story or a cosmologically elegant one, depending on how you look at it.

Nidavellir — also called Svartalfheim in some sources — is the underground realm where the dwarves live and work. Its geography is the geography of mines and forges: tunnels, caverns, the glow of furnaces, the ring of hammers on metal. It is a world of extraordinary productivity operating in permanent darkness.

Niflheim: The World of Mist and Ice

Niflheim is one of the two primordial realms that existed before the world was made — the world of mist and bitter cold from which the Élivágar rivers flowed into Ginnungagap. It is the oldest of the nine worlds, and in some sense the most fundamental, since its interaction with Muspelheim produced the conditions for everything else.

In the Viking Age sources, Niflheim and Hel are sometimes used interchangeably and sometimes treated as distinct realms adjacent to each other. Niflheim appears to be the broader territory — a vast, dark, cold region beneath the roots of Yggdrasil — while Hel is the specific domain within it where the dead reside. The confusion between the two is partly a product of the way the sources were written down, by Christian authors working with oral traditions that may not have been entirely systematic to begin with.

What is clear is that Niflheim is not a pleasant place. It is dark, cold, and located as far below Asgard as Asgard is above Midgard — a cosmological distance that suggests maximum separation from everything bright and warm and living. It is the destination of Níðhöggr, the dragon who gnaws at Yggdrasil's roots from below, and of the rivers that carry the worst of the dead — oath-breakers, murderers, those who died in ways that precluded Valhalla — to the shores of Hel.

Hel: The Realm of the Dead

Hel is both a place and a person — the realm of the ordinary dead and its ruler, a figure of the same name, daughter of Loki and the giantess Angrboða.

The goddess Hel is one of Loki's three monstrous children — sister to the Midgard Serpent and to the wolf Fenrir. Odin cast all three of them away when their potential for destruction became apparent: Jörmungandr into the ocean, Fenrir bound on an island, Hel sent to Niflheim to rule over the dead who did not qualify for Valhalla or Fólkvangr. Her appearance in the sources is described as half living and half dead — one side of her body the color and texture of normal human skin, the other dark and decomposing. She is not evil, exactly, but she is relentless. She takes what comes to her and does not give it back lightly.

The realm she rules reflects her character. It is described in the sources as surrounded by a high wall with a single gate, approached by a downward road that grows darker as it descends. A river called Gjöll — the one Hermóðr crosses during his mission to retrieve Baldr — runs along its border, its bridge guarded by a giantess named Móðguðr who asks the purpose of all who approach. The realm within is gloomy, cold, and quiet — not a place of torment in the Christian sense, but a place of absence, of the diminished continuation of a life that has been drained of its vitality.

This is crucial to understand. Hel is not hell. The Norse realm of the dead was not a punishment, and the people who ended up there were not condemned criminals or sinners. They were simply people who had not died in battle — the old, the ill, those taken by accident or disease. The Norse afterlife was not primarily moral in its structure. It was social: where you went when you died depended largely on how you died, not on how you had lived. A kind and generous person who died of fever went to Hel. A murderer who fell in battle might go to Valhalla. The apparent injustice of this was not a problem the Norse sources tried to resolve, because it was not understood as injustice — it was the nature of fate, and fate was not obligated to be fair.

The story of Baldr's death — which we will meet in the chapter on death and the afterlife — hinges on Hel's realm and on its ruler's one concession to negotiation: she will release Baldr if every being in creation weeps for him. Almost every being does. Loki does not. Baldr remains in Hel until after Ragnarök.

The Worlds Together

Nine worlds, arranged along the branches and roots of a single tree, connected by bridges and roads and the routes of those willing to make difficult journeys — this is the Norse cosmos in its basic structure, and it is worth stepping back to appreciate what kind of universe it is.

It is not a universe designed for human comfort. Humans live in its middle, not its heights. The forces most relevant to their daily lives — the elves, the dwarves, the giants pressing at the edges of the world — are present and active in ways that cannot be safely ignored. The dead are not gone but resident in a nearby realm, accessible to those with the skill and the courage to reach them. The end of everything is already encoded in the system: Níðhöggr is gnawing, Fenrir is bound and furious, the fire of Muspelheim is waiting.

What this cosmology offered its believers was not comfort but orientation. It told them where they were — in the middle of something vast and serious, connected to forces both above and below, responsible for maintaining their small portion of order against the chaos that surrounded it. It told them who their neighbors were, what those neighbors wanted, and how to conduct relationships with them. It told them that the world would end, and that knowing this was not a reason for despair but a reason for the specific kind of courage that lives alongside knowledge of its own futility.

The nine worlds are not a fantasy. They are a map — imprecise, contested, incomplete — of a reality that the Norse people believed they inhabited. Understanding that map is not an academic exercise. It is the necessary context for everything else this book has to say.

Chapter Eight

Gods, Goddesses, and Deities

The Norse gods are not like other gods.

This is not a claim about their power or their importance. It is a claim about their nature. The God of Christianity is omniscient, omnipotent, and perfect — a being so far beyond human comprehension that the distance between him and his creation is the fundamental fact of the religion. The gods of Norse Paganism are something else entirely. They are powerful, yes, and they know things that humans do not, and they can do things that humans cannot. But they are also hungry, lustful, frightened, petty, generous, grief-stricken, and mortal. They make mistakes with consequences they cannot undo. They pursue knowledge they do not have and wisdom they cannot guarantee will be enough. They will all die at Ragnarök, and they know it, and they go on anyway.

This is why they resonated with the people who worshipped them, and why they continue to resonate now. They are not perfect beings to be obeyed. They are flawed beings to be emulated — struggling, as humans struggle, against the limits of what they know and what they can control, and doing so with a degree of style that makes the struggle worth watching.

The Norse pantheon is large, and this chapter cannot be exhaustive. What it can do is introduce the gods most central to the tradition — the ones whose stories illuminate the values, the anxieties, and the cosmological thinking of the people who told them — and give each of them the attention they deserve.

The Two Tribes

The Norse gods are divided into two distinct groups, and understanding the division is essential to understanding the mythology.

The Aesir are the primary tribe — the gods of Asgard, whose principal qualities are sovereignty, war, wisdom, and law. Odin is their king. Thor is their champion. Tyr is their embodiment of justice. Frigg is their highest-ranking goddess. The Aesir represent the ordering principle of the cosmos: hierarchy, deliberation, the imposition of structure on chaos. They are the gods who build walls, establish councils, make binding oaths, and go to war when oaths are broken.

The Vanir are the other tribe — the gods of Vanaheim, whose principal qualities are fertility, nature, magic, and abundance. Freya is their most famous member. Freyr is their god of the harvest and the sun's warmth. Njord is their master of the sea and its wealth. The Vanir represent the generative principle of the cosmos: growth, cycles, the forces that operate below the level of deliberate control, the magic that works through relationship rather than command.

The two tribes were not always at peace, and the war between them — which we will discuss in its proper place — produced one of the most consequential exchanges in Norse mythology. But for most of Norse religious history, they coexisted and complemented each other, the Aesir and Vanir together constituting the full range of divine power that the cosmos required.

Odin: The All-Father

Odin is the most complex figure in the Norse pantheon, and possibly the most difficult to summarize without flattening him into something he is not.

He is the king of the Aesir, the ruler of Asgard, the father of Thor and Baldr and numerous other gods. He is associated with wisdom, poetry, war, death, magic, and the runic alphabet. He is called the All-Father — *Alfǫðr* — not because he created everything, but because he is the father or foster-father of most of the significant gods. He is also called the Wanderer, the One-Eyed, the Terrible, the High One, and approximately a hundred and fifty other names, which is itself a statement about how many different aspects of existence the Norse attributed to him.

His appearance in the sources is consistent: an old man, tall, wearing a broad-brimmed hat pulled low over one eye socket — empty because he gave the eye to Mimir in exchange for a drink from the well of wisdom that Mimir guards. He carries a spear named Gungnir, forged by the dwarves, that never misses its mark. He travels with two ravens named Huginn and Muninn — Thought and Memory — who fly across all nine worlds each day and return to whisper what they have seen into his ears. He rides an eight-legged horse named Sleipnir, the child that Loki bore in mare form, the fastest of all horses in the nine worlds.

The eye is the most important detail. Odin sacrificed it deliberately, knowing what it would cost, because the wisdom available at Mimir's well was worth more to him than his sight in that eye. This willingness to pay catastrophic prices for knowledge is the defining characteristic of Odin's mythology. He hung on Yggdrasil for nine days and nine nights, pierced by his own spear, to learn the runes. He gave himself to himself — a sacrifice to the god by the god — because the knowledge was locked behind a threshold that only death could open. He regularly consults the severed head of Mimir, preserved with herbs and magic, because access to Mimir's counsel is worth the strangeness of the arrangement.

What Odin is pursuing, with such relentless cost to himself, is knowledge of Ragnarök — specifically, knowledge of whether there is any way to prevent it or survive it. The answer, as far as the sources reveal, is no. The fate of the gods is woven, Fenrir will swallow him, and all his preparation has amounted to the ability to face what is coming with his eyes open. This does not stop him from trying. The tragedy of Odin is that he is the most knowledgeable being in the cosmos and it is not enough, has never been enough, and he has always known this.

He is also, in the accounts that survive, morally complicated in ways that monotheistic traditions rarely permit their highest deity. He cheats. He manipulates. He arranges the deaths of heroes he has favored, when their deaths serve his purposes at Ragnarök — drawing them into Valhalla to strengthen his army. He takes lovers, abandons them, and moves on with the pragmatism of someone who has decided that personal loyalty is less important than cosmic survival. He is not a god to be trusted with your secrets. He is a god to be respected, appeased, and approached with awareness that his interests and yours may not align as neatly as you would like.

For the Viking people, this complexity was not a defect. It was a recognition. The universe was not governed by a benevolent and consistent power. It was governed by something more like Odin — brilliant, knowledgeable, genuinely caring about certain things, and ultimately willing to sacrifice almost anything in pursuit of its own imperatives. Understanding this did not produce despair. It produced a particular kind of clear-eyed courage — the willingness to act well and bravely in a world that was not, at its highest levels, organized around your welfare.

Thor: The Defender

If Odin is the mind of the Norse pantheon — reflective, strategic, willing to endure any suffering for greater knowledge — Thor is its body. Where Odin thinks, Thor acts. Where Odin manipulates, Thor strikes. He is the god of thunder, of strength, of the protection of Midgard and its human inhabitants, and he is the most straightforwardly popular deity in the Norse world.

Thor is the son of Odin and the earth giantess Jörð — half god, half giant, a combination that gives him the divine authority of the Aesir and the raw physical power of the jötnar in a single enormous body. He is the largest of the gods, red-bearded, loud, possessed of a temper that the sources describe with a mixture of respect and affection, and armed with the most famous weapon in Norse mythology.

Mjölnir — Thor's hammer, forged by the dwarven brothers Sindri and Brokkr under circumstances that involved Loki's interference and a bet about which craftsmen were more skilled — is not just a weapon. It is a cosmological tool. It can destroy mountains. It can call down lightning. It can consecrate marriages and bless newborns and hallow the dead for their journey. When the Norse people hung small hammer pendants around their necks — as thousands of archaeological finds confirm they did — they were not simply expressing Viking identity. They were placing themselves under the protection of the power those hammers represented.

Thor's relationship with the giants is the most active and violent in the mythology. He travels to Jotunheim regularly — sometimes on diplomatic missions, more often on expeditions that end with giants dead and Thor somewhat satisfied. His battles with the giants are not merely entertaining, though they are often that. They are cosmologically functional: Thor is the force that keeps the world's borders intact, that prevents the chaos of Jotunheim from flooding into Midgard, that maintains the conditions under which human life is possible. Every time he kills a giant, he is doing the work that the world requires.

He is also, the sources make clear, not particularly clever. This is not presented as a failing — it is presented as part of his character, balanced by his enormous strength and his uncomplicated reliability. He is the god you want beside you when the giants arrive, and not necessarily the god you want making strategic decisions. The stories that involve Loki tricking Thor, or Thor being outwitted by particularly cunning giants, have a quality of fond exasperation about them — the acknowledgment that brute force, however necessary, is not sufficient for all situations.

His popularity across the Norse world was extraordinary and endured deep into the Christian period. When the missionaries arrived and the people of Scandinavia began adopting the new faith, the last thing they tended to let go of was Thor. The man who prayed to Christ at home and to Thor during a storm at sea was not confused. He was hedging his bets with the god who had, from his perspective, the most directly relevant track record.

Tyr: The Just

Tyr is one of the oldest gods in the Germanic pantheon — his name is cognate with the Latin *deus* and the Greek *Zeus*, suggesting that he was once a sky-father figure of enormous importance, the chief deity of an earlier religious layer that Odin eventually superseded. By the Viking Age, he had been repositioned within the mythology, his role narrowed and his stories reduced to a handful. What remained was vivid.

Tyr is the god of law, justice, and single combat — the deity you invoked before a duel, before a legal proceeding, before any situation in which the outcome was meant to be determined by something more principled than naked force. Tuesday is his day, a linguistic survival that testifies to the era when his importance was unquestioned.

His defining story is the binding of Fenrir. The wolf Fenrir — Loki's son, growing larger every day, already too powerful for any chain the gods could forge — could only be bound with a magical ribbon called Gleipnir, made by the dwarves from impossible things: the sound of a cat's footsteps, the beard of a woman, the roots of a mountain, the sinews of a bear, the breath of a fish, the spittle of a bird. Gleipnir looked like silk and was unbreakable.

Fenrir, understandably suspicious of an unbreakable ribbon that looked like silk, agreed to be bound only if one of the gods would place a hand in his mouth as a guarantee of good faith. No god was willing to do this except Tyr. He placed his right hand — his sword hand — between Fenrir's teeth. The ribbon held, Fenrir was bound, and Tyr lost his hand.

The story is usually told as a demonstration of Tyr's courage, and it is that. But it is also a demonstration of something more specific: the willingness of the principle of justice to pay the cost that justice requires. The binding of Fenrir was necessary for the safety of the cosmos. Someone had to be willing to pay for it personally. Tyr understood this, accepted the cost, and did what was needed. That he did it with full knowledge that the wolf would take his hand makes the gesture not less rational but more so — a sacrifice made in clarity rather than ignorance, which is the most demanding kind.

He will fight Fenrir again at Ragnarök. They will kill each other.

Heimdall: The Watchman

Heimdall stands at the edge of Asgard, at the top of the Bifrost where it meets the realm of the gods, and watches.

He is the sentinel of the Norse cosmos — the god whose function is vigilance, whose identity is defined entirely by the quality of his attention. He needs less sleep than a bird. He can hear grass growing in the fields and wool growing on sheep. He can see as far as one hundred miles in any direction, in full darkness or full light. He holds the Gjallarhorn — the great horn whose sound, when blown, will signal the beginning of Ragnarök and summon the gods to their final battle.

He is watching for the giants. He is always watching for the giants.

Heimdall's mythology is sparse compared to Odin's or Thor's — he has no great cycle of adventures, no defining sacrifice, no complex web of relationships with other figures. He is present at the edges of stories rather than at their center. But his presence matters, because a cosmos without Heimdall would be a cosmos without warning, and a cosmos without warning is a cosmos that cannot even defend itself against what is coming.

There is a version of the Norse creation myth in which Heimdall, disguised as a mortal named Rígr, fathered the three classes of human society: the thralls, the free farmers, and the nobility. In this account, social hierarchy is not a human invention but a divine plan, built into the world by a god who understood that order required differentiation of roles. Whether this represents a genuine ancient tradition or Snorri Sturluson's attempt to systematize Norse society through mythological narrative is a question scholars continue to debate. What it reveals, regardless of origin, is the Norse assumption that the structure of society and the structure of the cosmos were the same kind of thing.

At Ragnarök, Heimdall and Loki will fight and kill each other — a pairing whose logic is cosmological: the principle of vigilance and the principle of deception, the watchman and the trickster, locked in a final cancellation.

Loki: The Trickster

Loki is the most written-about figure in the Norse pantheon after Odin, and the most difficult to categorize.

He is not a god of the Aesir by birth — his father was the giant Fárbauti and his mother was Laufey, whose name and nature are themselves sources of ongoing scholarly dispute. He is not a giant either, exactly, though he shares their blood and their capacity for shape-shifting and their tendency to operate outside the rules that govern the more straightforwardly divine. He exists at the boundary between categories, which is where tricksters always live, and his presence in any story signals that the boundaries are about to be tested.

Loki is clever in the way that makes people uncomfortable — not wise, not strategic in any long-term sense, but possessed of a lateral intelligence that can find solutions no one else has thought of and create problems no one anticipated. He is the reason the gods have many of their most important treasures. He commissioned Mjölnir, Gungnir, and Draupnir from the dwarves through a combination of bet-making and follicular sabotage. He helped build Asgard's wall. He rescued Thor's hammer from the giant Þrymr through a cross-dressing scheme of considerable elaborateness. When the gods needed something impossible, Loki was often the one who produced it.

He is also the reason for many of the gods' greatest losses. He caused the death of Baldr. He fathered the Midgard Serpent, Fenrir, and Hel — the three most dangerous beings in the cosmos — on a giantess named Angrboða. He engineered the circumstances that bound him to opposing the gods at Ragnarök, where he will steer the ship of the dead against Asgard and fight Heimdall to mutual destruction.

The question of whether Loki is ultimately good or evil is one that the sources refuse to answer, because it is not the right question. Loki is neither. He is uncontainable — a force that serves whatever interest is most compelling to him in the moment, with an honesty about his own nature that the more conventionally heroic gods do not always share. He makes mischief because mischief is interesting. He helps the gods because they are his companions and their problems are entertaining challenges. He destroys Baldr because Baldr's perfection is, in some deeply felt way, intolerable to him.

After Baldr's death, the gods punish Loki in terms that have no parallel in the mythology for severity: he is bound beneath the earth, a serpent dripping venom on his face, his wife Sigyn holding a bowl to catch it. When the bowl fills and she turns away to empty it, the venom falls on him, and his writhing causes earthquakes. He will remain there until Ragnarök breaks his bonds.

The cruelty of this punishment says something about how seriously the gods took what he did. Loki had always been unreliable, always been dangerous, always operated at the edge of what the community could tolerate. Baldr's death was the moment the community decided it had tolerated enough.

Frigg: The Queen of Asgard

Frigg is Odin's wife, the highest-ranking goddess of the Aesir, and one of the most frustratingly underdocumented figures in the entire tradition.

She is associated with marriage, motherhood, domestic life, and prophecy. She sits beside Odin on the high seat Hliðskjálf, which means she too can see across all nine worlds — but where Odin acts on what he sees, relentlessly and at great cost, Frigg is described in the sources as keeping her knowledge to herself. She knows, according to one account, the fate of all beings, but she does not speak of it. Whether this is wisdom, grief, or simply the character of a goddess who has lived beside the most restless mind in the cosmos long enough to understand the limits of intervention is left, like so much in Norse mythology, to the reader's interpretation.

Her most fully realized story is the death of Baldr — the event around which the entire mythology pivots toward its ending. Her attempt to protect her son by extracting oaths from every substance in creation is both the most devoted act of motherhood in the Norse tradition and, because of the single oversight with the mistletoe, the mechanism of his death. She is the most careful of mothers in a cosmos that punishes excessive care with the specific cruelty of giving you exactly what your carefulness missed.

The relationship between Frigg and Freya has occupied scholars for generations. Their names are similar. Their attributes overlap significantly — both are associated with love, fertility, magic, and the choosing of the dead. Both are described as having traveling husbands whose absences leave them lonely.

Some scholars have argued that they are originally the same goddess, later differentiated. Others maintain that they were always distinct. The sources do not resolve this definitively, which is frustrating for anyone who likes clean answers and entirely characteristic of the Norse tradition, which rarely provides them.

Freya: Love, War, and Magic

Freya is a Vanir goddess who was sent to Asgard as part of the hostage exchange after the war between the two divine tribes, and who became, over time, one of the most important deities in the entire Norse pantheon.

She is the goddess of love, beauty, fertility, gold, and magic — specifically seiðr, which she is said to have taught to Odin. She is also a goddess of war: she receives half of all warriors who fall in battle, choosing first from among the dead before Odin takes the rest. She brings them to her hall Fólkvangr — the Field of the People — which the sources suggest was at least as desirable a destination as Valhalla, though less is written about it. She rides into battle in a chariot pulled by two large cats. She owns a cloak of falcon feathers that allows its wearer to fly. She has a necklace called Brísingamen, the most beautiful object in the nine worlds, which she obtained from four dwarves in circumstances the sources record with an explicitness that later Christian scribes clearly found uncomfortable.

She weeps gold tears when she is separated from her husband Óðr — whose name is so similar to Óðinn that the relationship between them has never been satisfactorily explained. Óðr travels constantly, as Odin travels constantly, and Freya searches for him, and the searching is part of her character: she is a goddess who knows loss as intimately as she knows love, and who continues pursuing both regardless.

The Prose Edda records that her name was once used as an insult — that she had been with every god and elf in Asgard, that her sexuality was a scandal rather than an expression of her divine nature. This tells us something about the Christian context in which the Prose Edda was written rather than anything reliable about Freya's actual mythology. A goddess of love who is also a goddess of magic and war does not fit neatly into the categories available to a medieval Christian author, and the discomfort shows.

What the pre-Christian Norse thought of Freya is better inferred from the evidence of worship. She was widely venerated — her name appears in place names across Scandinavia, her attributes appear in grave goods and votive offerings, and the accounts of her ritual role in the Aesir-Vanir conflict suggest that her power within the divine community was genuine and substantial. She was not a peripheral figure. She was a queen of a different kind from Frigg — less concerned with order and marriage and the proper conduct of the household, more attuned to the forces that operate beneath order, through desire and fate and the magic that moves in the blood.

Freyr: The Lord of Summer

Freyr is Freya's twin brother, a Vanir god who was sent alongside her to Asgard after the war, and one of the most important deities in the Norse tradition for the people whose survival depended on good harvests.

He is associated with sunshine, rain, fertility of the land and of people, prosperity, and good seasons. The Uppsala temple that Adam of Bremen described in the eleventh century — the last great center of Norse Pagan worship — placed Freyr at the center of its three great idols, flanked by Odin and Thor. This tells us something about his relative importance to the agricultural communities of Sweden, for whom a god who could be asked to make the harvest good was at least as pressing a concern as a god who could be asked to make the raids successful.

Freyr's defining story is his falling in love with the giantess Gerðr — a story that begins with him sitting on Odin's forbidden throne Hliðskjálf and seeing her across the worlds, her arms so radiantly bright that they lit the sky and sea. He became so consumed by desire that he refused to eat or sleep, and eventually sent his servant Skírnir to court her on his behalf. Skírnir succeeded — through a combination of gifts, threats, and a curse of such terrible specificity that the sources record it with evident relish — but the price Freyr paid was his sword, given to Skírnir as payment. The sword that fought giants on its own, by itself, without anyone needing to wield it.

This is the sword he will not have at Ragnarök, when Surtr comes from Muspelheim with fire. He will fight the fire giant with a stag's antler, which is not sufficient, and he will die. He knew, when he gave the sword away, or should have known, what the cost of that gift would eventually be. He gave it anyway, for love of Gerðr. Whether this is romantic or tragic or both is a question the Norse sources leave open, as they tend to with the questions that matter most.

The Valkyries

The Valkyries are among the most recognizable figures in Norse mythology and among the most misunderstood.

In popular culture — from Wagner's operas to contemporary fantasy — they tend to appear as warrior women of superhuman beauty, armored, mounted on flying horses, selecting the brave dead and carrying them to Valhalla. This is not entirely wrong, but it is incomplete in ways that matter.

The name *Valkyrja* means "chooser of the slain" — and choosing was, in the original conception, a more active process than simply selecting the already-dead. The Valkyries were understood to influence the outcome of battles, not merely to observe them. They moved across the battlefield during the fighting, determining who would fall and who would survive, weaving the fate of the engagement with a literalness that connects them to the Norns and to the practice of seiðr. The Old Norse poem *Darraðarljóð* — "The Song of the Spear" — describes twelve Valkyries weaving on a loom whose warp threads are men's intestines, whose weights are human heads, whose shuttle is an arrow. They are not observers of war. They are its operators.

They serve Odin specifically — they are his agents in Midgard, carrying out his instructions about which warriors should die and which should live to fight another day. The warriors they select are carried to Valhalla, where they become the einherjar — the chosen dead who feast and fight each day in preparation for Ragnarök. The Valkyries serve them mead in the hall at night, which has given them their most persistent image in later tradition.

Individual Valkyries appear in the sources with names that encode their function: Göndul means wand-wielder, Skuld shares her name with one of the Norns, Geirskögul means spear-shaker. Several Valkyries appear in the heroic poetry as lovers of mortal heroes — Brynhildr, the most famous, is a Valkyrie punished by Odin for defying his wishes in a battle, put into an enchanted sleep surrounded by fire, and eventually woken by the hero Sigurðr, with consequences that drive the entire Völsunga cycle of tragedy. The love stories of the Valkyries tend to end badly, which is possibly a function of what happens when beings whose job is to decide who dies fall in love with people who are capable of dying.

The War Between the Aesir and the Vanir

The conflict between the two divine tribes is one of the oldest and most cosmologically significant stories in the Norse tradition, and it begins, like so many Norse stories, with someone bringing an unwelcome gift to Asgard.

The figure responsible was a Vanir woman named Gullveig — a practitioner of seiðr, a wielder of magic so powerful and so disruptive that the Aesir, confronted with it, did not know whether to be amazed or terrified. The sources suggest they settled on terrified. Odin ordered her killed. She was stabbed with spears and burned — and rose from the fire. She was burned again, and rose again. She was burned a third time, and rose a third time, and walked out of the hall under a new name: Heiðr, the Shining One, distributing her magic wherever she went, loved by wicked women and praised by evil wives, according to the Poetic Edda's pointed description.

The attempt to destroy what the Aesir did not understand — and its failure — sparked the war. The Vanir, learning what had been done to one of their own, prepared for battle. Odin threw his spear into the Vanir host — the traditional gesture that opened a battle — and the two tribes fought across the plains between their realms.

The war produced no winner. The Aesir could not overcome the Vanir's magic. The Vanir could not overcome the Aesir's military strength. After a period of mutual destruction that reduced the walls of Asgard to rubble, both sides came to the same conclusion simultaneously: this was not worth continuing. They sat down and talked.

The peace agreement that ended the war was sealed in the Norse fashion: both sides spat into a vessel, and from the mixed saliva they created a being. His name was Kvasir, and he was the wisest being in the cosmos — the product of two opposed tribes deciding to create something together that neither could create alone. Kvasir traveled the nine worlds answering questions, and was eventually killed by two dwarves who drained his blood into vessels and mixed it with honey to create the Mead of Poetry — whoever drank it gained the ability to compose perfect verse. The mead passed through several hands before Odin stole it back, which is why Odin is the god of poetry as well as everything else.

The hostage exchange that followed the peace agreement was the other significant consequence of the war. The Vanir sent Njord and his children Freyr and Freya to Asgard. The Aesir sent Hœnir and Mimir to Vanaheim. The arrangement soured quickly: Hœnir, though impressive in appearance, proved incapable of making decisions without Mimir's counsel, and when Mimir was absent the Vanir found themselves with a leader who stared blankly at every problem. Concluding they had been cheated, the Vanir beheaded Mimir and sent the head back to Odin. Odin preserved it with herbs and gave it the power of speech, and kept it close as his most trusted counselor. The presence of a severed but talking head in Odin's inner circle was apparently not unusual enough to require comment.

The war between the Aesir and the Vanir is sometimes read as a mythological memory of the encounter between two different human cultures — the warrior aristocracy and the agricultural communities — and their eventual synthesis. The historian Mike Greenberg has noted the parallels with the historical contact between the Norse and Sami peoples, the warriors and the shamans, and argued that the myth encodes a real process of cultural negotiation. Whether or not that reading is correct, the war's outcome is clear: the two tribes merged, the magic of the Vanir became part of the Aesir's repertoire, and the combined pantheon that emerged was richer and more complete than either tribe had been alone.

The gods that resulted from this synthesis — Aesir and Vanir living together in Asgard, sharing their different gifts — are the gods the Vikings worshipped. They are complicated, contradictory, occasionally at odds with each other, and collectively more than capable of facing what the cosmos requires of them.

Almost.

Chapter Nine

Rituals and the Norse Calendar

Religion, for most of human history, has not been primarily a matter of belief. It has been a matter of practice — of what you do, when you do it, and how you do it in company with the people around you. The Norse Pagans had beliefs, certainly: about the gods, the nine worlds, the nature of fate, and the shape of the cosmos. But what held those beliefs in place, what made them real rather than merely intellectual, was the rhythm of ritual that structured the year.

The Norse sacred calendar was not a list of holidays. It was a framework for living — a series of moments at which the boundary between the human world and the divine one became permeable, at which the gods could be addressed directly, the dead could be acknowledged, and the community could remind itself of what it was and what it owed to the forces that sustained it. Miss enough of these moments, and the relationship between the human world and the divine one would begin to fray. Maintain them, and the world would continue to function as it was meant to.

Understanding this calendar is essential to understanding Norse Paganism not as a museum piece but as a living practice — one that shaped the daily and seasonal experience of the people who followed it, and that continues to shape, in modified forms, the experience of those who follow it today.

The Structure of the Norse Year

The Norse year was not divided as ours is. The modern calendar, inherited from Rome and refined by centuries of Christian liturgical practice, divides the year into twelve months of roughly equal length, with fixed dates for fixed observances. The Norse year was organized differently — around the solar cycle and the agricultural realities of Scandinavian life, with major festivals clustered at the moments of transition between seasons.

The primary division was between winter and summer. Winter began at what we would call mid-October and ended at what we would call mid-April. Summer occupied the remaining six months. This was not an arbitrary distinction. In Scandinavia, winter was genuinely dangerous — the period when food stores were tested, when animals needed shelter, when the darkness lasted long enough to feel like a permanent condition. The transition between seasons was an event, not just a calendar notation, and it was marked accordingly.

Within this basic structure, three major festival periods organized the religious year: Dísablót in late winter, marking the approach of the growing season; Sigrblót in mid-spring, marking the beginning of summer and the raiding and traveling season; and the great midwinter festival — Yule — marking the darkest point of the year and the sun's return. Around these three anchors, smaller observances and household rituals filled the months, connecting the individual and the family to the larger cycles of the cosmos.

Blót: The Sacrificial Feast

Before we can discuss the individual festivals, we need to understand the central ritual mechanism that gave them their structure and their power: the blót.

The word *blót* — from which the modern Scandinavian words for blood derive — referred to the sacrificial feast that was the primary form of Norse religious observance. A blót was an offering to the gods or to other supernatural powers, made in a communal context, with food and drink as the central elements. It was simultaneously a sacrifice, a feast, and an act of relationship maintenance between the human community and the divine powers it depended on.

The mechanics of a blót varied with context and scale. At the largest public level — the great seasonal blóts held by kings and chieftains at the major festivals — animals were sacrificed, their blood collected in bowls called *hlaut-boðlar* and applied with twigs to the walls of the temple and the bodies of the participants. The meat was cooked and eaten communally, with the understanding that the gods were present at the feast, honored by the offering and sharing in the abundance it created. Ale and mead were blessed and consumed as part of the same ritual, each drinking horn dedicated to a specific deity or purpose before being passed around the gathering.

At the household level — where most actual religious practice took place, away from the grand temples and the royal festivals — a blót might involve nothing more elaborate than the setting aside of a portion of food and drink at mealtimes, or the offering of something valued into a fire, a well, or a body of water. The principle was the same: an acknowledgment that what you had was not entirely yours, that the powers that made abundance possible had a claim on a portion of it, and that honoring that claim was what kept the relationship functional.

The word the Norse used for this exchange is instructive. They called it *gefa til* — to give toward — and the preposition carries the weight of the concept. You gave toward the gods, toward a future of continued favor, toward the maintenance of a relationship that could not be allowed to lapse. Gift exchange in the Norse world was never simply generosity. It was always also obligation, reciprocity, and the deliberate cultivation of bonds that might otherwise dissolve.

Yule: The Midwinter Festival

Of all the observances in the Norse calendar, Yule — *Jól* in Old Norse — was the most elaborate, the most important, and the most stubbornly persistent. It is also, of all the Norse festivals, the one whose traces are most visible in the modern world, embedded so deeply in the cultural fabric of northern

Europe that even a millennium of Christianity and several more centuries of commercial repackaging have not entirely obscured its origins.

Yule was a midwinter festival lasting twelve days, centered on the winter solstice — the longest night of the year, after which the sun begins its gradual return. For people who lived through Scandinavian winters, the solstice was not an astronomical abstraction. It was a threshold: the point at which darkness stopped gaining and light began its slow recovery. The relief of this transition was worth marking, and marking seriously.

The religious dimensions of Yule were extensive. It was primarily associated with Odin — the *Jólnir*, the Yule-figure, the hooded wanderer who moved through the world at midwinter in ways that blurred the boundary between the divine and the human. The Norse imagined Odin riding across the sky during the twelve nights of Yule on his eight-legged horse Sleipnir, accompanied by the spirits of the dead and a retinue of supernatural beings — a procession known as the *Wild Hunt* in later Germanic tradition. Children left their boots near the hearth or on rooftops for Sleipnir, filled with hay and carrots, and hoped to find them filled with gifts in the morning. The echoes of this in the modern tradition of leaving shoes out for Saint Nicholas, or hanging stockings for a gift-bearing figure who travels by night, are not coincidental.

The Yule feast itself was extraordinary by the standards of Viking Age life. Large animals — particularly boars, sacred to Freyr — were slaughtered and consumed over the twelve days. Ale was brewed specially for the festival and blessed in the name of the gods. Toasts — *minni*, memory-drinkings — were raised to Odin for victory, to Njord and Freyr for good harvests and peace, and to the memories of dead kinsmen. The fires were kept burning throughout the twelve nights — a practice whose practical function of providing warmth and light during the darkest period of the year was inseparable from its ritual significance of maintaining the human hearth against the darkness pressing in from outside.

The Yule log — a massive piece of wood brought into the hall and burned slowly over the festival period, its remnant kept to kindle the following year's fire — was the material center of the domestic celebration. The continuity it represented was literal: fire carried from one year into the next, the household's warmth maintained across the coldest threshold. It was also cosmological: human fire maintained in correspondence with the sun's fire returning, the microcosm of the hearth reflecting the macrocosm of the seasonal cycle.

Yule was also a time when the boundary between the living and the dead was considered particularly thin. Ancestor spirits were believed to return during the twelve nights, visiting the homes they had known and the families that had descended from them. Food and drink were left out for these returning dead — a practice that persisted in Scandinavian folklore long after the formal religious observance had been replaced by Christmas. The combination of feasting, gift-giving, fire-tending, and communion with the dead made Yule not just a festival but a comprehensive ritual renewal of the community's relationships with every level of the supernatural world.

When Christianity arrived in Scandinavia, the church did not attempt to abolish Yule — it absorbed it, replacing its divine associations with the Nativity while preserving its timing, its twelve-day structure, its emphasis on feasting and gift-giving, and most of its material practices. The Norse name persisted in the Scandinavian languages. The log persisted in northern European tradition. The twelve days persisted as the liturgical structure of Christmastide. The figure who traveled by night delivering gifts to children persisted, in modified form, into the modern era. Yule is the festival that Christianity tried hardest to replace and succeeded least in erasing.

Dísablót: The Festival of the Dísir

In late winter — around what we would now call February — the Norse held the Dísablót, a festival dedicated to the *dísir*: female spirits associated with fate, protection, and the fertility of the coming season.

The dísir are difficult to define precisely, because the Norse sources use the term in ways that are not always consistent. At their most specific, they are the female ancestral spirits of a family line — the women of previous generations who retained, after death, a protective interest in their descendants and a capacity to influence the family's fortune for good or ill. At their most general, they encompass a broader category of feminine supernatural power that includes the Norns, the Valkyries, and the beings associated with particular geographical locations.

What united these various manifestations was their connection to fate and to the domestic and agricultural fertility of the household. The dísir were not distant cosmic forces. They were local, specific, personal — tied to a particular family, a particular piece of land, a particular inheritance. Keeping them properly honored was an intimate obligation, carried out in the home rather than in public temples, by the women of the household rather than by official priests.

The Dísablót was the annual observance at which this relationship was formally renewed. A feast was prepared, offerings were made, and the dísir were invited to participate in the abundance that the household had managed to accumulate through the winter. The ritual was explicitly feminine in its management — the sources suggest that the women of the household took primary responsibility for its conduct — and it was emphatically private. When Christian missionaries encountered the Dísablót, they found it among the most tenacious of all Norse ritual survivals, precisely because it took place behind closed doors, in the domestic sphere where their authority was weakest.

The timing of the Dísablót at the end of winter carried agricultural logic. As the growing season approached, the household's relationship with the forces that determined whether the coming year would be abundant or meager needed to be in good order. The dísir could be asked to bless the seeds, the animals, the fertility of the land — and their continued benevolence was worth the cost of a feast.

Sigrblót: The Feast of Victory

As winter gave way to spring — around what we would now call late April or early May — the Norse celebrated Sigrblót: the sacrifice for victory, the festival that opened the summer season and blessed the undertakings that summer made possible.

Summer in Viking Age Scandinavia was the season of activity. The ships were relaunched. Trading voyages departed. Raids were planned and executed.

Agricultural work intensified as the growing season demanded everything available. Sigrblót was the ritual preparation for all of this — the moment at which the community asked the gods for favor in the ventures it was about to undertake.

The primary deity associated with Sigrblót was Odin — unsurprisingly, given his association with war, victory, and the outcomes of battle. Sacrifices made at Sigrblót were oriented toward success in conflict: the safety of those going raiding, the defeat of enemies, the accumulation of the wealth and reputation that summer expeditions were meant to produce. But agricultural blessing was also requested, because the same season that allowed raiding also allowed farming, and the community needed both.

The feast that accompanied Sigrblót shared the structure of the Yule blót — communal eating, blessed ale, memorial toasts — but its atmosphere was different. Where Yule was oriented inward, toward the household and the ancestral dead, Sigrblót was oriented outward, toward the wider world and the opportunities it offered. It was the festival of departure and ambition, the moment at which the Norse community committed itself to what the summer would demand of it and asked the gods to make the demand worthwhile.

Haustblót: The Harvest Sacrifice

At the other end of summer — as the harvest was brought in and the days began to shorten — the Norse held Haustblót: the autumn sacrifice, the festival of gratitude and preparation.

Where Sigrblót asked the gods for what the summer might bring, Haustblót thanked them for what the summer had actually produced, and asked for their continued support through the winter to come. It was a feast of abundance, held at the moment when that abundance was most visible — the grain in storage, the animals fat from summer pasture, the year's hunting and fishing yielded and preserved.

The three primary deities honored at Haustblót were Odin, Njord, and Freyr — representing respectively the martial success of the summer's raiding, the maritime success of the trading voyages, and the agricultural success of the harvest. This triad reflects the economic realities of Viking Age Scandinavia, where no single form of livelihood was sufficient and the community's prosperity depended on success across multiple domains simultaneously.

Haustblót also marked the beginning of the period in which the dead became more present. As winter approached and the world contracted toward its darkest point, the boundary between the living and the dead thinned. The Haustblót feast included offerings to ancestors — the recognition that the living and the dead shared an interest in the community's continued prosperity, and that the dead's goodwill was as worth cultivating as the gods'.

Álfablót: The Sacrifice to the Elves

Alongside the great seasonal blóts, the Norse observed a series of smaller, more private rituals directed not at the gods but at other supernatural powers. The most distinctive of these was the Álfablót — the sacrifice to the elves — held in mid-autumn, around the same time as Haustblót.

The Álfablót was a household ritual of unusual privacy. Unlike the great seasonal blóts, which were communal affairs held at temples or on the estates of powerful chieftains, the Álfablót was conducted within the home, by the family, for the family. Strangers were not welcome — the sagas record instances of travelers being turned away from households during the Álfablót, told that the household was closed to outsiders for the duration. Even the Christian missionaries who systematically documented Norse religious practice found the Álfablót difficult to observe, precisely because it was so consistently hidden from them.

The elves who were honored at the Álfablót were understood to be intimately connected to the fertility of the land and to the well-being of the people who worked it. They were associated with the ancestors — the connection between elves and the honored dead is present throughout the saga literature — and with the generative power of the specific place in which the household was located. Keeping the elves well-disposed required regular acknowledgment, regular offering, and the kind of private, personal attention that the great public festivals, oriented toward the distant gods, could not provide.

This combination of intimacy, privacy, and connection to both the dead and the land made the Álfablót the festival most resistant to Christianization. It had no public face to replace, no temple to demolish, no priest to silence. It was simply a family, in their own home, honoring the powers they depended on. This is the kind of practice that persists across religious transitions not because it is hidden deliberately but because it is so embedded in daily life that it does not register as a distinct religious act to those who practice it.

The Sumbel: The Ritual Toast

Not every Norse ritual was tied to the agricultural calendar. Some were social occasions that carried their own ritual weight — moments at which the community defined itself through the act of speaking together.

The most important of these was the *sumbel* — a ritualized drinking ceremony in which participants took turns holding a horn of ale or mead and speaking formally before drinking. The speeches made during a sumbel were not casual conversation. They were performative in the deep sense: what was said in a sumbel had a quality of permanence and commitment that ordinary speech did not. Boasts made during a sumbel were obligations. Oaths sworn in a sumbel were binding. Praise offered to gods or ancestors during a sumbel was understood to reach its recipients.

The structure of a sumbel typically involved three rounds of toasting. The first was dedicated to the gods — Odin, Thor, and Freyr being the most commonly named. The second was dedicated to heroes and ancestors — the dead whose lives had defined the community's values and whose example the living were expected to follow. The third was open: participants could boast of their own accomplishments, make vows about what they intended to do, or praise anyone they chose.

The sumbel was not a party. It was a mechanism for the production and maintenance of social identity — a formal occasion at which the community's values were stated aloud, confirmed by shared drinking, and committed to by the act of speaking before witnesses. What was said in the sumbel became part of the record, in a society that had no written records in the modern sense, through the memories of everyone who heard it. This made the sumbel simultaneously an oath-taking ceremony, a memorial service, a legal proceeding, and a feast.

The modern Asatru communities we will meet in the next chapter have revived the sumbel with considerable fidelity to its original form — recognizing, correctly, that the ritual's power derives from its social rather than its supernatural dimensions, and that those dimensions remain fully functional in the present day.

Sacred Spaces and the Hof

The Norse did not, in the early centuries of their religious practice, build dedicated temples in the way that the Greeks or Romans did. The earliest Norse ritual spaces were natural — groves of particular trees, bodies of water, rock formations with unusual characteristics, hilltops from which the landscape could be seen in all directions. The concept of the *vé* — a sacred enclosure, a place set apart from ordinary space — could be applied to any location that had been consecrated through use and acknowledgment.

As Norse society became more complex and more stratified, dedicated ritual buildings — called *hof* — began to appear. The hof was typically a large hall, built on the model of the longhouse, with the major idols of the gods installed inside and a raised area for sacrificial activities. Adam of Bremen's description of the Uppsala temple is the most detailed account we have, but archaeological evidence for hof-like structures has been found across Scandinavia, suggesting that dedicated ritual space was a regular feature of the Viking Age religious landscape.

The management of the hof was typically the responsibility of a *goði* — a priest-chieftain figure whose religious and political authority were not distinguished in the Norse understanding. The goði conducted the sacrifices, maintained the temple, organized the seasonal festivals, and represented the community in its relationship with the gods. The role was hereditary in many communities, passing within families along with the land and the political authority that went with it.

Women also held ritual authority in the Norse world — the völva as a traveling specialist in seiðr, the women of the household as the primary managers of the domestic observances, and the *gyðja* — the female counterpart of the goði — as a ritual leader in her own right. The sources give us fewer details about the gyðja than about the goði, partly because the Christian authors who documented Norse religious practice were more comfortable writing about male religious authority, and partly because female ritual leadership operated more consistently in the private domestic sphere that Christian documentation found hardest to penetrate.

The Thread That Runs Through Everything

What is striking, looking at the Norse ritual calendar as a whole, is how thoroughly it integrated the different dimensions of Norse life.

The seasonal festivals addressed the agricultural cycle, the raiding and trading calendar, the relationship with the dead, and the maintenance of the gods' favor — all simultaneously, because these were not separate concerns but facets of a single unified existence. A farmer who was also a raider, who also venerated his ancestors and kept faith with the local elves and made offerings to Freyr at planting time and Odin at the summer's end — this was not a person with compartmentalized religious practices. This was a person whose entire life was organized within a religious framework that made sense of all of it together.

The modern practitioners of Norse Paganism who have revived these festivals — as we will see in the next chapter — have had to do so in circumstances that are radically different from those in which the festivals originated. They do not farm. They do not raid. They may not live near their ancestors' graves or in landscapes that carry the accumulated sacred weight of centuries of use. What they have recovered, or are trying to recover, is not the specific cultural context of Viking Age Scandinavia but the underlying logic: that the year has a shape, that the shape matters, that marking it together with intention and honoring the forces that sustain existence is both meaningful and necessary.

That logic is older than the Viking Age. It was already present in the Sami drumbeats we encountered in the first chapter, in the Bronze Age burial mounds filled with offerings, in the bog deposits of the Iron Age where the Norse put their most valuable things into the earth and the water as gifts to powers they could feel but not see. The rituals changed as the culture changed. The impulse behind them never did.

CHAPTER TEN

Death and the Afterlife

The Norse did not fear death the way many traditions teach their followers to fear it. They did not ignore it either. What they did was something more interesting than either: they thought about it with the kind of sustained, unflinching attention that produces genuine theology rather than mere consolation, and they arrived at a picture of what comes after life that is richer, stranger, and more honest about the human condition than most traditions permit themselves to be.

The Norse afterlife is not a single place. It is a system — a set of destinations determined not by the moral quality of your life but by the manner of your death, with different realms offering different conditions, different company, and different roles in the drama that will eventually end everything. Understanding this system requires setting aside the instinct to look for the heaven and the hell — the reward and the punishment — that monotheistic traditions have made the default framework for imagining what comes next. The Norse cosmos does not sort the dead into the deserving and the condemned. It sorts them by function, by fate, and by the specific circumstances of the moment when their thread was cut.

Valhalla: The Hall of the Slain

Valhalla is the most famous address in Norse mythology, and it deserves its reputation — not because it is the most pleasant destination available to the dead, though it has its compensations, but because it is the destination most freighted with cosmological purpose, the one whose existence explains something fundamental about why the Norse understood bravery in battle as a religious act rather than merely a social virtue.

The hall itself is described in the Poetic Edda with a specificity that suggests genuine imaginative investment. Its roof is made of shields, its rafters of spears, its walls hung with coats of mail. It has five hundred and forty doors, each wide enough that eight hundred warriors could march through abreast. These numbers are not meant to be taken literally — they are the Norse poetic idiom for incomprehensible scale, for a space that could contain the army required for what is coming. The hall is enormous because it needs to be enormous. It is being filled, one dead warrior at a time, in preparation for Ragnarök.

The warriors who dwell in Valhalla are called the *einherjar* — the chosen slain — and their existence there is structured around the dual purpose they serve. During the day they fight: they arm themselves, form into companies, and battle each other across the plains outside the hall with the full lethal force they possessed in life. Those who fall are killed as completely as they can be killed, wounds real and painful, the experience of dying genuinely experienced. By evening, they are whole again — wounds healed, lives restored — and they return to the hall for the feast that Odin provides.

The feast is extraordinary even by the standards of the Norse imagination of abundance. The meat comes from a boar named Sæhrímnir, killed each night by the cook Andhrímnir, cooked in a cauldron called Eldhrímnir, and restored to life each morning to be killed again. The mead flows from the udder of the goat Heiðrún, who feeds on the leaves of Yggdrasil and produces enough to fill vessels that the sources describe as inexhaustible. The Valkyries serve the feast, moving among the einherjar with drinking horns, attending to their needs with a combination of divine grace and military efficiency.

This daily cycle — battle and feast, wounds and renewal, death and resurrection — is not entertainment. It is training. The einherjar are being prepared for the day when Heimdall's horn sounds across the nine worlds and Odin leads them out of Valhalla to fight the giants at Ragnarök. They will die in that battle — finally, truly, permanently — but they will die as the best warriors the world has ever produced, honed by years of daily combat into something that no living army could match. The purpose of Valhalla is to produce the army that will face the end of the world.

This reframes what it meant, for a Viking warrior, to die in battle. It was not merely an occupational hazard or an honorable conclusion to a fighting life. It was recruitment — selection by the Valkyries for a specific cosmological role, a continuation of the warrior's function in a new theater with stakes higher than any earthly conflict. The man who fell at Lindisfarne or on a Frankish riverbank was not simply dead. He was being taken to Valhalla to train for the last battle. His death was a beginning as much as an ending, and the courage it took to face it was inseparable from the religious understanding that made it meaningful.

It is also worth noting what Valhalla is not. It is not peaceful. It is not restful. It is not the cessation of struggle. For a culture that understood struggle as the defining condition of existence, an afterlife without it would not have been appealing — it would have been a punishment disguised as a reward. Valhalla offers the Viking warrior exactly what he valued most in life: good company, adequate food, and something worth fighting for. The fact that the fighting never stops is the point, not the problem.

The Valkyries as Choosers

We met the Valkyries in the previous chapter as figures of battle and fate. Here it is worth dwelling on their specific role in the passage between life and death, because it shapes everything about how the Norse understood the warrior's death.

The Valkyries did not simply collect the already-dead from battlefields. They were present during the fighting, moving through the chaos of combat, determining which warriors would fall and which would survive. This was an active exercise of the divine power over fate — a direct intervention in the events of Midgard by agents of Odin, carrying out the instructions he had formed based on his partial, agonized, incomplete knowledge of what Ragnarök would require.

A warrior chosen by the Valkyries was not chosen randomly. He was chosen because Odin needed him — because something in his fighting capacity, his spirit, or the specific skills he carried made him valuable for the purpose that Valhalla served. This gave the Norse warrior a framework within which his individual death could be understood as meaningful on a cosmic scale. He was not just a man who happened to be in the wrong place when a spear was thrown. He was a man selected by the divine intelligence of Asgard for a role in the war that would end the world.

The Valkyrie's arrival at the moment of death is described in the sources with a vividness that suggests genuine imaginative engagement with the experience of dying in battle. They appear mounted, armed, magnificent — beings of power and beauty whose presence at the threshold between life and death transformed that threshold from an ending into a transition. To see a Valkyrie was to know that your death was chosen rather than accidental, that you were going somewhere rather than simply ceasing.

Fólkvangr: Freya's Field

Not all the honored dead went to Valhalla. Freya received her half.

Fólkvangr — the Field of the People — is described as a meadow over which Freya presides, selecting her portion of the battle-slain before Odin takes his. The poem *Grímnismál* records this arrangement in a single verse, with a brevity that suggests it was common knowledge rather than an obscure tradition: Freya chooses half the slain every day, and Odin has the other half.

The sources say almost nothing about what Fólkvangr is like or what existence there involves. Freya's hall within it, Sessrúmnir, is described only as large and beautiful — a characterization that tells us the essentials without any of the vivid detail that makes Valhalla so imaginatively present. Some scholars have suggested that Fólkvangr was understood as essentially equivalent to Valhalla — that Snorri Sturluson, working from multiple oral sources of varying age and reliability, preserved a distinction between the two that may have been more nominal than substantive in actual practice. Others maintain that they were genuinely different destinations, serving different purposes in the cosmological plan.

What seems clear is that Freya's claim on half the battle-dead was not a marginal arrangement but a central feature of the Norse understanding of death in battle. The goddess of love and magic and the weavings of fate had as much authority over the disposition of the honored dead as the god of war and wisdom. This says something important about the Norse conception of what dying well actually required — not just martial capacity, but the approval of forces associated with beauty, fertility, and the deeper currents of fate that run beneath the surface of any battle.

Hel: The Realm of the Ordinary Dead

Most people did not die in battle. They died in their beds, of illness or old age, or in accidents, or of the thousand ordinary failures of a body living in a difficult world. For these people — the majority of the Norse dead — the destination was Hel.

We have already described Hel's geography in the chapter on the nine worlds: the downward road growing darker as it descends, the high fence surrounding it, the gate, the river Gjöll, the giantess Móðguðr at the bridge, and the realm within — gloomy, cold, quiet, presided over by the goddess of the same name whose body is half living and half dead. What we have not yet done is follow the dead into that realm and see what existence there actually looked like.

The sources are sparse on this, which is itself significant. Valhalla is described in loving detail because it served a purpose the Norse were deeply invested in understanding. Hel is described in general terms because its inhabitants had no great cosmic role, no army to fill, no battle to prepare for. They were simply there — continuing some diminished form of the existence they had known in life, in a place that was neither paradise nor torment but something more like a permanent twilight.

The Norse understanding of Hel reflects a broader pattern in their thinking about death: the idea that the dead remain present, remain connected to the living, and retain something of the identity and condition they carried at the moment of death. A person who died sick might spend their existence in Hel still sick. A person who died wealthy might maintain their social position among the dead as they had among the living. The dead could be spoken to — the seiðr practitioners and the völur could reach them through their trances — and they retained knowledge of the world they had left that made them useful to consult.

This is why the Norse tended their dead with such care. Burial goods were not merely symbolic — they were provisions, genuine gifts to the dead person for use in the existence ahead. A woman buried with her loom weights was being equipped for a continued life in which weaving would still be part of her daily experience. A warrior buried with his weapons was being sent to Hel with the tools of his identity, so that what he had been in life would not be stripped from him in death. The care taken in these burials was, from the Norse perspective, an act of practical provision as much as an act of grief.

The Ship Burial and Other Funerary Rites

The Norse buried their dead in ways that varied considerably by region, period, and social status — and studying those variations tells us as much about Norse beliefs as any written source.

The most spectacular funerary practice was the ship burial, in which the dead person was placed inside a full-sized vessel — sometimes accompanied by horses, dogs, servants, and extraordinary quantities of grave goods — and either buried in the earth or, in some accounts, set alight and pushed out to sea. The Oseberg ship burial in Norway, excavated between 1904 and 1905, is the most richly preserved example: a ninth-century burial containing two women, one of whom may have been a völva or a queen of high status, surrounded by sledges, beds, a decorated cart, kitchen equipment, textiles, and personal objects of remarkable quality.

The logic of the ship burial reflects the Norse understanding of the afterlife as a journey rather than an arrival. The ship was transportation — the vehicle that would carry the dead person to wherever they were going, across whatever waters separated the world of the living from the world of the dead. In a culture that understood the sea as the primary medium of travel and the ship as the technology that made the world accessible, placing the dead in a ship was giving them the most powerful means of conveyance available.

Not everyone received a ship. The expense and logistics involved made ship burials the prerogative of the wealthy and powerful. The more common funerary practices involved burial mounds of varying sizes — earthen constructions that ranged from simple covered graves to elaborate chambered mounds containing entire room-settings — and cremation, in which the body was burned and the ashes interred, sometimes with grave goods that had been burned alongside the dead person.

The Arab traveler Ibn Fadlan, who encountered Norse traders on the Volga River in 922 C.E., left an eyewitness account of a Viking ship cremation that is the most detailed external description of Norse funerary practice in existence. His account describes the preparation of the ship, the dressing of the dead chieftain in his finest clothes, the killing of a horse, dogs, hens, and a slave woman who volunteered to accompany her master in death, and the final burning of the entire assemblage. Ibn Fadlan was horrified by what he witnessed and fascinated by it simultaneously, and his description has the quality of genuine reportage — an outsider trying to make sense of something profoundly alien to his own cultural framework while recording it with the precision of a man who understood he was seeing something important.

What his account confirms is that the Norse understood death as a passage that needed to be properly equipped and properly witnessed — that the transition between the world of the living and the world of the dead was serious enough to require ceremony, sacrifice, and the explicit participation of the community in sending the dead person off correctly.

The Death of Baldr

If there is a single story in the Norse tradition that illuminates every dimension of the Norse understanding of death — its theology, its emotional weight, its political implications, and its relationship to the fate of the cosmos — it is the death of Baldr.

Baldr is Odin's son by Frigg, and he is, by universal agreement among gods and humans alike, the most beloved of all the Aesir. He is described with a consistency across the sources that is unusual: beautiful, radiant, generous, wise, gentle, his presence a source of joy to everything and everyone around him. The grass grows more green where he walks. The other gods love him without reservation, which in a mythology full of divine rivalries and divine grudges is itself a kind of miracle.

Then the dreams began.

Baldr started having nightmares — specific, recurrent, detailed visions of his own death. In a world where dreams were understood as communications from the spirit world rather than as neurological noise, this was serious. The gods gathered to discuss what could be done, and Odin, too alarmed to trust any consultation available in Asgard, mounted Sleipnir and rode down the long road to Hel.

He arrived to find a feast prepared — tables set, mead poured, the hall decorated in a way that could only mean it was waiting for a guest of honor. He found a völva buried in a mound nearby and raised her from the dead to question her, an act that cost him something the sources do not specify but that the act of raising the dead always costs. She told him what he needed to know and did not want to hear: the feast was for Baldr. The hall was being prepared for Odin's son. What was coming could not be stopped.

Frigg responded to this news with the most comprehensive protective action in the mythology. She traveled across the nine worlds and extracted an oath from every substance, every plant, every animal, every stone, every disease, every poison, every force of any kind — an oath that none of them would harm Baldr. The effort was extraordinary and the result appeared to be complete. To test it, the gods began throwing things at Baldr — stones, weapons, fire — and watching everything bounce off harmlessly. The game became a source of delight, a demonstration that the most beloved of the gods had been made invulnerable.

There was one oversight. Frigg had not asked mistletoe to swear the oath, because it seemed to her too small and too young and too harmless to be worth the trip.

Loki found this out through a conversation with Frigg in disguise. He found a sprig of mistletoe, shaped it into a dart, and brought it to where the gods were playing their game of throwing things at Baldr. He found the blind god Höðr standing apart from the celebration, unable to participate. He offered to help — to guide Höðr's aim so that he could join the fun. He placed the mistletoe dart in Höðr's hand. He pointed his arm in Baldr's direction.

Höðr threw. The dart flew. Baldr fell dead.

The silence that followed is one of the most effective moments in the Poetic Edda — a silence that the poem describes with a restraint that makes the grief fully present rather than explained. The gods stood and said nothing. Then the grief broke, and it was total. Only Loki did not weep.

Frigg, composing herself with a visible effort, asked if anyone would ride to Hel and offer whatever the goddess there required in exchange for Baldr's return. Hermóðr — one of Odin's sons — volunteered. He took Sleipnir and rode for nine days and nine nights through valleys so dark that he could see nothing, until he reached the bridge over Gjöll and convinced the giantess guarding it to let him pass.

He found Baldr in Hel's hall — pale, seated in the place of honor, the guest of honor at the feast Odin had witnessed being prepared. He spoke with him, spent the night, and in the morning presented his request to Hel herself.

The goddess's response was careful. She would release Baldr on one condition: every being in creation must weep for him. If a single being refused, he would stay.

Hermóðr rode back to Asgard with the terms. Messengers were sent across the nine worlds to ask everything — gods, humans, giants, animals, stones, trees, even the metals in the earth — to weep for Baldr. Everything wept. The grief was genuine and universal, because Baldr had been genuinely and universally loved.

In a cave, disguised as a giantess named Þökk, Loki refused. His refusal was brief and brutal: let Hel keep what she has. The messengers returned to Asgard with the news. Baldr remained in Hel.

The story does not end there. It continues through Loki's capture and his terrible punishment beneath the earth, through the cosmic ripples that Baldr's death set in motion, all the way to Ragnarök — where Baldr, surviving the destruction of the cosmos, will return to the new world that rises from the ashes. His death was not the final word. It was the pivotal event that set the countdown to the final word in motion.

What the story tells us about the Norse understanding of death is layered and precise. It tells us that even the gods can die, that the most beloved being in the cosmos is not protected by his belovedness, and that the agent of death is not malice but a combination of oversight, vulnerability, and the specific personality of Loki — which is to say that death arrives through the cracks in whatever protection we have built, through the one thing we forgot to ask, through someone we trusted at the wrong moment. It tells us that grief is the appropriate response to death, and that a grief so total it encompasses all of creation is not hyperbole but accurate calibration. And it tells us that death is not the end of the story, that even in Hel the identity of the dead is preserved, and that the cosmos has plans for Baldr that extend beyond the moment of his dying.

Other Fates of the Dead

Beyond Valhalla, Fólkvangr, and Hel, the Norse imagined several other destinations for the dead, each connected to the specific circumstances of a person's death.

Those lost at sea — a real and constant possibility in a culture of seafarers for whom the ocean was the primary means of travel and trade — were understood to go to the underwater realm of Rán and Ægir. Ægir was a giant of the deep ocean, a brewer of extraordinary ale whose hall hosted feasts attended by the Aesir gods; Rán was his wife, a being of more sinister aspect who was said to drag drowning travelers down to her hall with a net. Together they ruled the ocean's depths, and together they received the dead who died there.

The relationship between these ocean giants and the drowned dead was, like so many Norse arrangements, ambivalent. Rán's nets were not understood as punishment — she was not malicious so much as possessive, claiming what the ocean claimed. And Ægir's hall, whatever its proximity to death, was described as a place of feasting and abundant mead — not entirely unlike Valhalla in its broad outlines, if considerably wetter. For a people who accepted drowning as one of the ordinary possible conclusions of a life at sea, having a coherent cosmological framework for where the drowned went was not a luxury but a necessity.

Those who died by illness or old age went to Hel, as we have seen. But within Hel's realm, the social distinctions of life apparently persisted: the dead of high status occupied better positions than the dead of low status, and the treatment they received in life — the quality of their burial, the richness of their grave goods, the care with which their kin sent them off — influenced the conditions of their existence in the realm of the dead. This gave the living a genuine practical stake in providing well for their dead, which is one of the reasons Norse funerary archaeology is so rich. The grave goods were not merely symbolic. They were understood to function.

There were also those who did not make it to any of the established afterlife destinations — the *draugr*, the restless dead who returned to haunt the places they had inhabited in life. The draugr appears throughout the saga literature as a figure of genuine menace: a dead person whose death had been in some way improper, whose burial had been inadequate or cursed, or whose attachment to life was too strong to release them toward whatever came next. They were physically present — not ghosts in the modern sense but corporeal undead, capable of violence and requiring physical confrontation to subdue. The saga heroes who dealt with draugr did so by entering their burial mounds and wrestling them — a task that required extraordinary courage, since the draugr were often stronger in death than they had been in life, and since the inside of a burial mound was not a forgiving combat environment.

The draugr represents the failure case of the Norse funerary system: what happens when the dead are not properly sent off, when the transition between life and death is not managed with the care and attention the system requires. Properly buried, properly mourned, properly equipped with the tools and goods of their former life, the Norse dead were expected to make their way to wherever they were going and stay there. The draugr was the consequence of getting it wrong — a reminder that the living had real obligations to the dead, and that failing in those obligations produced real consequences.

Ragnarök and the Question of Renewal

The Norse afterlife cannot be understood without Ragnarök, because Ragnarök is the event toward which the entire system of post-death destinations is oriented.

Valhalla exists to fill with warriors. Those warriors exist to fight the fire giants when the world ends. The einherjar train daily for a battle they know is coming and know they will lose. The gods go to that battle knowing their individual fates — Odin swallowed by Fenrir, Thor poisoned by Jörmungandr, Freyr dying without his sword, Tyr and Fenrir killing each other, Heimdall and Loki canceling each other out — and they fight anyway, because the alternative to fighting is simply waiting for the end to arrive without resistance.

This is the Norse theology of death in its most compressed form: everything ends, the ending is certain, and the appropriate response to that certainty is not despair but the fullest possible engagement with the time available. The gods do not find meaning in survival — they cannot survive Ragnarök, and they know it. They find meaning in the quality of what they do before the ending arrives, in the courage and the generosity and the continued maintenance of the world's order against the chaos pressing in from Jotunheim.

The human warrior who fell in battle and went to Valhalla was participating in this same logic. His death was not a tragedy to be minimized. It was a role to be fulfilled — a contribution to the cosmic effort that all of Asgard was engaged in, the slow, impossible, necessary work of holding things together until the moment when holding things together was no longer possible.

After Ragnarök, the sources tell us, something new rises from the ashes. The earth surfaces from the water. Two humans who sheltered in the branches of Yggdrasil — Líf and Lífþrasir, Life and Life's Desire — descend and repopulate the world. Several gods survive, including Baldr, who returns from Hel, and Thor's sons Móði and Magni, who inherit their father's hammer. The new world is green and abundant, the catastrophe of the old one cleared away, a fresh beginning for whatever comes next.

This is the eschatological hope that Christianity, with its own narrative of death and resurrection and new creation, found easiest to work with when it arrived in Scandinavia — and the Christian missionaries who encountered the Ragnarök narrative were not wrong to see in it something they recognized. The Norse cosmos ends badly and begins again. The gods die and some of them return. The world is destroyed and renewed. The structure is not identical to the Christian story of death and resurrection, but the family resemblance was close enough to provide a bridge, and the missionaries used it.

What did not transfer was the specific Norse understanding of what the ending meant in the time before it arrived. For the Norse, Ragnarök was not primarily a promise of renewal. It was primarily a fact of structure — the built-in consequence of a cosmos made from violence, maintained against entropy, and populated by beings whose conflicts were too fundamental to be permanently resolved. The renewal that followed was real, but it was secondary. The courage required to live well in a world you knew was ending — that was primary. That was what the whole system, the whole calendar of ritual, the whole elaborate cosmology of nine worlds and Yggdrasil and Norns and Valkyries and einherjar, was designed to support.

It is a remarkable thing to have built. And it is, in its way, an honest thing — a theological system that does not promise more than it can deliver, that looks at the facts of existence and says: yes, it ends. Yes, the gods die. Yes, the world is destroyed. And here is how to live in the light of that, with generosity and courage and the specific joy of people who know that what they have is temporary and have decided, in full awareness of that fact, to value it anyway.

Chapter Eleven

Conversion Paths

Norse Paganism should not exist.

By every measure of historical probability, it should have disappeared completely — absorbed into Christianity during the eleventh century along with the temples, the sacrificial practices, and the public rituals that had given it visible form, and survived only as folklore, as etymology, as the faint mythological residue that persists in the names of weekdays and the plots of superhero films. Religions that lose their institutional infrastructure rarely recover it. The historical record is full of belief systems that were suppressed, assimilated, or simply outlived by the cultures that practiced them, and that are now accessible only through archaeology and textual analysis — known to scholars, invisible to everyone else.

Norse Paganism did not follow this pattern. It contracted, certainly. It lost its temples and its public festivals and its goðar and its institutional presence in the life of Scandinavian society. But it did not disappear. It went underground — into households, into oral tradition, into the literary preservation that Snorri Sturluson and the anonymous poets of the Eddas provided — and it waited. And in the nineteenth century, in the twentieth century, and with increasing momentum into the twenty-first, it returned.

The people who practice Norse Paganism today are not a curiosity or a historical re-enactment society. They are a genuine religious community — or rather several communities, organized around different approaches to the same ancient tradition, with different emphases and different relationships to the source material. Understanding who they are and how they practice requires understanding the paths that Norse Paganism has developed as it has rebuilt itself for a world that looks nothing like the one in which it originated.

The Question of Reconstruction

Before we meet the modern practitioners, it is worth pausing on the challenge they face — because it is a genuine and interesting one, and the various ways different communities have responded to it account for much of the diversity within contemporary Norse Paganism.

The problem is this: the religion being practiced today is not a continuous tradition. There is no lineage of priests who have transmitted the rites and the theology intact from the Viking Age to the present. The chain was broken — by Christianity, by time, by the catastrophic loss of the institutional structures that would have preserved the living practice of the religion rather than just its literary record. What modern practitioners have access to is a body of texts — the Eddas, the Sagas, the runestones, the archaeological evidence — from which a practice must be reconstructed rather than simply continued.

Reconstruction is not the same as invention, but it is not the same as recovery either. It requires interpretation, and interpretation requires choices, and choices have consequences for what the resulting practice looks and feels like. How literally should the mythological texts be read? How much can archaeology tell us about ritual practice, and how much has to be inferred? How do you adapt practices designed for an agricultural, seafaring, raiding society to the lives of people who live in cities and work in offices? How do you handle the parts of the tradition that are ethically uncomfortable by contemporary standards — the slavery, the violence, the rigid gender hierarchies?

Different communities within modern Norse Paganism have answered these questions differently, and the answers have produced genuinely distinct paths — each with its own emphases, its own relationship to the source material, and its own understanding of what it means to practice a Norse Pagan religion in the present day.

Asatru: True to the Aesir

Asatru is the largest and most visible of the modern Norse Pagan paths, and in many ways the one that has done the most to define what contemporary Norse Paganism looks like to the outside world.

The name means, straightforwardly, "true to the Aesir" — a commitment to the worship of the Aesir tribe of gods, with Odin, Thor, Freya, and their companions at the center of the practice. It emerged as a formal religious movement in the nineteenth century, during the period of romantic nationalism that swept northern Europe and produced, among other things, Wagner's operas, the revival of interest in medieval Scandinavian literature, and a widespread desire to reconnect with what was imagined as the authentic pre-Christian culture of the Germanic and Nordic peoples. Iceland formally recognized Asatru as an official religion in 1973 — the first time a Norse Pagan faith had received legal recognition anywhere since the conversion, roughly nine centuries earlier.

What Asatru actually looks like in practice varies considerably by community, but certain elements are consistent enough to constitute something like a common core. The blót — the ritual feast and offering — is the primary form of worship, performed at the major festivals of the Norse calendar and at other occasions when contact with the divine seems necessary or appropriate. The sumbel is the primary form of communal gathering, with its three rounds of toasting to the gods, the ancestors, and whatever the participants choose to honor. The gods are understood as living beings — not metaphors, not Jungian archetypes, not symbols of natural forces, but actual entities with whom a genuine relationship is possible and worth cultivating.

The Nine Noble Virtues — courage, truth, honor, fidelity, discipline, hospitality, industriousness, self-reliance, and perseverance — are the ethical framework most commonly associated with American Asatru, developed in the 1970s as a way of translating the values implicit in the Norse mythological tradition into a modern code of conduct. They bear some resemblance to the virtues celebrated in the heroic poetry — the qualities that made a Viking warrior worthy of reputation and respect — adapted for a world in which the relevant arena is more likely to be a workplace than a battlefield. Not all Asatru communities embrace them with equal enthusiasm, and some find the explicit codification alien to the spirit of a tradition that communicated its values through stories rather than commandments.

The kindred — the local worship community — is the basic social unit of Asatru practice. Kindreds vary in size from a handful of households to congregations of hundreds, and they vary in formality from loose networks of friends who meet for festivals to organizations with formal membership, hierarchical leadership, and established ritual procedures. Some kindreds are affiliated with national or international organizations — the Asatru Folk Assembly and the Troth are the two largest in the United States — while others operate independently, defining their own practices and their own relationships to the wider community.

One of the ongoing debates within Asatru — the one that has caused the most friction and produced the most explicit organizational divisions — is the question of who the religion is for. A minority within the movement has argued that Asatru is specifically the religion of people of northern European ancestry, that its gods and its traditions belong to a particular ethnic heritage, and that this ethnic dimension should shape membership in the community. The majority position, increasingly clearly stated by the major organizations, is that Norse Paganism is a path open to anyone drawn to it, regardless of ancestry — that the gods choose their worshippers rather than the other way around, and that ethnic gatekeeping is both theologically unsound and practically repugnant. This is not merely an internal disagreement. It has produced genuine splits in the community, formal statements of principle from the major organizations, and ongoing effort to define what contemporary Norse Paganism stands for as a matter of values rather than genetics.

The Asatru communities that have navigated this question most successfully have done so by returning to what the tradition actually emphasizes: hospitality, honor, courage, generosity. These are not ethnic virtues. They are human ones, available to anyone willing to practice them.

Vanatru: True to the Vanir

Vanatru emerged in the early 1990s as a distinct path within the broader Norse Pagan community — a recognition that for some practitioners, the

Vanir gods spoke more clearly and more personally than the Aesir, and that their relationship with those gods deserved a framework that honored its specific character.

The name means "true to the Vanir," and the path centers on Freya, Freyr, Njord, and the other deities associated with fertility, nature, magic, and the earth's generative power. Where Asatru tends toward the communal, the structured, and the martial — reflecting the Aesir's own qualities — Vanatru tends toward the personal, the intuitive, and the earth-centered. It is a path more oriented toward individual spiritual experience than toward group ritual, more connected to the cycles of the natural world than to the community of warriors, more likely to emphasize the magic and the mystery of the tradition than its heroic and martial dimensions.

The ritual structure of Vanatru shares much with Asatru — blót, sumbel, the Norse calendar — but the specific deities honored, the specific aspects of those deities emphasized, and the overall atmosphere of practice differ in ways that practitioners find meaningful. A Vanatru blót for Freyr at planting time has a different quality from an Asatru blót for Odin before a battle — not because the ritual mechanics are different, but because the intention and the relationship are different. Vanatru practitioners tend to describe their relationship with the Vanir gods in terms of intimacy and reciprocity rather than petition and honor — a closeness that reflects the Vanir's own qualities of fertility and connection.

The ritual specific to Vanatru that has no direct Asatru parallel is the antler-walk — a practice in which the practitioner circles the sacred space carrying an antler, acknowledging Freyr and the spirit of the land in a gesture that is simultaneously a hallowing and an invocation. The antler is sacred to Freyr, given to Skírnir as part of the bride-price for Gerðr, and its use in ritual connects the practitioner to the most defining story of the god they are honoring.

Vanatru is not a separate religion from Asatru in any organizational sense — the paths are not mutually exclusive, and many practitioners engage with both the Aesir and the Vanir, adjusting their emphasis based on what a particular moment in their lives or the year's cycle seems to require. The Norse tradition itself makes no sharp division: the gods live together in

Asgard, the two tribes have been integrated since the war that ended in their exchange of hostages, and the worship of the whole pantheon was the norm rather than the exception in the Viking Age. Vanatru is better understood as an emphasis within the broader tradition than as a competing alternative to it.

Rökkatru: True to the Rökkr

At the darker edge of the Norse Pagan spectrum, Rökkatru takes as its focus the beings that most other paths treat as adversaries or peripheral figures: the Rökkr — the dark gods, the forces of chaos and destruction that the Aesir spend so much of their energy containing.

Hel, the goddess of the ordinary dead. Loki, the trickster whose arc through the mythology ends in the unraveling of everything. Fenrir, the wolf who will swallow Odin at Ragnarök. Jörmungandr, the serpent encircling the world. Surtr, the fire giant who will burn it. These are the beings that Rökkatru practitioners orient toward — not because they celebrate destruction, but because they recognize that the forces these figures represent are real, necessary, and deserving of acknowledgment.

The theological argument underlying Rökkatru is straightforward once stated: the Norse cosmos requires both order and chaos. The Aesir represent order; the Rökkr represent chaos. But chaos is not simply evil — it is the condition of change, of ending, of the clearing away that makes renewal possible. Ragnarök is not only a catastrophe. It is a transformation. The Rökkr who bring it about are not villains in any simple sense. They are agents of a process that is built into the structure of the cosmos, necessary for what comes after.

Practitioners of Rökkatru work with these beings in the same spirit that Asatru practitioners work with the Aesir — through ritual, through relationship, through the cultivation of a genuine connection with specific divine figures. Hel is approached as a guide through grief and loss, a power that can help with mourning, with the acceptance of endings, with the parts of life that other traditions are too comfortable to address directly. Loki is approached as a catalyst, a force for change in situations where change is needed but resisted

— which is to say, in most significant situations anyone faces. The serpent and the wolf are approached as reminders that nothing lasts, that the world's destruction is already encoded in its structure, and that living well requires making peace with that fact rather than pretending otherwise.

Rökkatru is not universally welcomed in the broader Norse Pagan community. Loki in particular is a divisive figure — the Troth, the major American Heathen organization, has at various times excluded his worship from its official rituals, on the grounds that his mythology makes him an enemy of the gods rather than a legitimate focus of devotion. The counterargument, advanced by Rökkatru practitioners and by the Lokeans we will meet shortly, is that excluding Loki from Norse Paganism requires ignoring a significant portion of the mythology, that the Norse tradition itself does not present him as simply evil, and that a religion which only honors the comfortable parts of its cosmology is not being honest with its source material.

This debate reflects something genuine about the nature of the tradition being reconstructed. Norse mythology is not a comfortable body of texts. It contains beauty and brutality, divine generosity and divine betrayal, gods who are genuinely admirable and gods who are genuinely appalling, and a cosmological structure that ends in total destruction. A Norse Paganism that smooths all of this into something universally reassuring would not be Norse Paganism. It would be something else, made from Norse parts, but arranged to serve a different purpose.

Lokeans

Lokeans are practitioners whose religious focus falls specifically on Loki — not as one deity among many but as the primary figure of their practice, the god whose nature and mythology most deeply resonates with their own experience and understanding of the world.

This requires some explanation, because Loki is the most controversial figure in the Norse pantheon for reasons that go beyond his role in Baldr's death and Ragnarök. He is a shape-shifter, a liar, a boundary-crosser, a figure who cannot be neatly categorized as either ally or enemy, as either good or evil, as either divine or monstrous. He is the father of the three most dangerous beings in the cosmos and the mother of Odin's horse. He helped build Asgard's wall and then helped bring it down. He saved the gods from consequences he had created and created consequences from which no one could save them. He is, in short, a figure who demands a certain kind of psychological courage to approach — the willingness to sit with ambiguity, to honor a force that cannot be controlled or predicted, to find meaning in chaos rather than despite it.

Lokeans tend to be, by the community's own description, intensely individual in their practice. Where Asatru emphasizes the kindred and the communal blót, Lokean practice is often solitary — a personal relationship with a specific deity, developed through private ritual, meditation, and the kind of intense theological engagement that comes from working with a figure who does not offer easy answers. Many Lokeans have found the internet an essential community space, connecting with others who share their focus in a broader landscape where they are often unwelcome or regarded with suspicion.

The Lokablót — the festival dedicated to Loki, held on April 1 — is the primary communal observance of the Lokean path. It involves offerings that Loki is understood to favor: fire, glittering objects, things that are changeable and unpredictable. The date is significant — the association of April Fools' Day with trickery makes it an apt celebration of a deity whose primary characteristic is exactly that. The humor is deliberate and the devotion behind it is genuine.

What Lokeans find in their relationship with Loki varies considerably. Some find in him a patron of change and transformation — a force that disrupts what has become too comfortable or too rigid. Some find in him a figure who models the experience of being marginalized, misunderstood, and punished for being genuinely different. Some find in him simply the most interesting figure in the mythology — the one whose stories are the most complex, whose motivations are the least reducible to simple categories, whose presence in any narrative immediately raises the stakes.

The Troth's ongoing debate about whether to welcome Loki into its official rituals reflects the genuine difficulty of integrating a figure this disruptive into an organized religious community. Loki does not cooperate with organizational agendas. He does not respect hierarchies or stay within the categories assigned to him. A community that officially honors him is a community that has committed to something genuinely unpredictable, and not everyone finds that appealing. The Lokeans who pursue their practice outside the major organizations may simply be accepting what working with this particular deity requires: a path that cannot be fully institutionalized, because the deity at its center will not allow it.

What These Paths Share

Despite their differences — in the deities they honor, in the communities they build, in the specific practices they employ — the paths within contemporary Norse Paganism share a common orientation that distinguishes them from most other religious options available in the modern world.

They are reconstructionist in method: they take seriously the obligation to engage with the historical and literary evidence, to know the Eddas and the Sagas and the archaeological record, to ground their practice in something more than personal preference. This does not mean they are rigid — the reconstruction project necessarily involves interpretation and adaptation — but it means they understand themselves to be in conversation with a real tradition rather than simply inventing something new.

They are polytheist in theology: the gods are many, real, distinct from each other, and individually worth relating to. This is a more demanding theological position than it might appear. It requires learning who the gods are, what they care about, what they have done, and what they might want from a relationship with a specific human practitioner. It requires the cultivation of genuine relationships rather than the performance of generic religious observance.

They are community-oriented in practice: even the most solitary practitioners understand themselves to be part of a broader tradition, connected to other practitioners across time and geography, inheriting something from those who practiced before them and responsible for passing it on to those who come after. The sumbel's three rounds of toasting — to the gods, the ancestors, and the living community — express this orientation in its most compact form.

And they are, in their best expressions, honest about the tradition they are inheriting — its beauty and its difficulty, its rich mythology and its ethically complex history, its vision of a cosmos that is magnificent and temporary and worth caring for anyway.

The Continuing Conversation

Norse Paganism's revival is not complete. It is ongoing — a conversation between practitioners, scholars, and the source material itself, conducted in real time, in communities spread across the world, with no central authority to resolve disputes and no final text to settle questions.

This is appropriate. The original tradition did not have a central authority either. The Norse religious world was decentralized — local, community-based, managed by goðar whose authority was practical rather than doctrinal — and the modern revival reflects this in its own decentralization, its multiplicity of paths and organizations and individual approaches.

What the revival demonstrates, above all else, is that the tradition survived. The nine hundred years between the Christianization of Scandinavia and the formal recognition of Asatru in Iceland were not a death but an interruption — a period during which the stories were preserved in books, the values were encoded in folklore and in the structure of the languages that developed from Old Norse, and the impulse toward a religion that took seriously the complexity of the cosmos and the difficulty of living well within it waited for conditions that would allow it to express itself again.

Those conditions arrived. They are still here. The conversation continues — in kindreds in Iceland and America and Australia and Brazil, in online communities that connect practitioners across distances the Viking Age could not have imagined, in the scholarship that continues to illuminate what the sources actually say and what they might mean, and in the individual experiences of people who have found, in these ancient stories and these old gods, something that speaks to the life they are actually living.

The Norse gods, as we observed at the end of the previous chapter, are difficult to kill.

The evidence, at this point, seems conclusive.

Chapter Twelve

The Thread That Remains

Every book about the past is really about the present. The questions we choose to ask of history, the details we linger on, the connections we draw between ancient belief and contemporary life — these are never neutral. They reflect what we are looking for, which reflects what we feel we are missing, which reflects something true about the moment we are living in.

Norse Paganism has returned to visibility precisely because the modern world has produced conditions in which it speaks to something real. A tradition that takes complexity seriously — in its gods, in its cosmology, in its unflinching account of how the world ends — has a particular appeal to people who have grown tired of traditions that promise more certainty than the evidence supports. A religion that honors the natural world as sacred, that builds community around shared ritual and shared obligation, that measures virtue by what you do rather than what you believe — these are not small things to offer a world that is, by various measures, running short of all of them.

But this book has not been primarily an argument about the present. It has been an account of the past, and it is worth returning to that past one final time — not to summarize what we have covered, but to hold it whole for a moment before setting it down.

What Was Built

The tradition we have explored in these pages was built over thousands of years, by people who left us almost nothing in writing and almost everything in objects — tools and weapons and jewelry and ships and the carved stones they set up at crossroads and beside rivers and on the edges of their fields to mark what mattered and warn against what threatened.

It began, as nearly as we can tell, with the Sami people and their shamanic relationship with a landscape that offered them survival in exchange for constant, intelligent attention. The noaidi with their drums, their trances, their negotiations with the spirit world — these were the first practitioners of what would eventually become Norse Paganism, developing in conversation with a different tradition that was moving in from the south as the North Germanic peoples settled the peninsula.

It matured through the Bronze Age, when trade routes brought Scandinavia into contact with the wider world and the wider world's ideas, when amber bought bronze and bronze bought social complexity, when the dead were buried with objects that expressed a belief in continuation rather than cessation. The Sun Chariot from Trundholm is not just a beautiful object. It is a theological statement about the relationship between the divine and the natural world, made three and a half thousand years ago, and it connects directly to what the Vikings believed when they carved Mjölnir on their runestones.

It deepened through the Iron Age, as trade routes collapsed and Scandinavia turned inward, becoming more self-reliant, more internally complex, developing the social structures and the agricultural practices and the religious institutions that would characterize the Viking Age. The gods began to take their recognizable forms during this period, their names appearing in inscriptions, their attributes taking shape in the material record.

It reached its fullest expression in the Viking Age itself— not the Hollywood version of horned helmets and mindless violence, but the genuine article: a society of farmers and traders and raiders and explorers who organized their lives around a cosmology of extraordinary sophistication, who worshipped gods who struggled and failed and tried again, who marked the turning of the year with feasts and offerings and the careful maintenance of relationships with every level of the supernatural world, who sent their dead off with provisions for the journey ahead and kept faith with the ancestors who had gone before them.

And then, over a hundred and fifty years of gradual, contested, never-quite-complete conversion, it was pushed underground — into households and oral traditions and the literary preservation of men like Snorri Sturluson, who understood that what he was recording was irreplaceable and wrote it down accordingly.

What Was Lost

We should be honest about what the conversion cost, because the loss was real and in some respects permanent.

The living practice of the religion — the temples, the goðar, the seasonal blóts conducted publicly with the participation of the whole community, the accumulated wisdom of practitioners who had spent lifetimes developing their understanding of the tradition — was gone within a few generations.

What survived was the literary record, which is not nothing, but which is also not the same thing. A description of how a ritual felt from the inside is not the same as the ritual. A poem about a god is not the same as a relationship with that god developed through years of worship and offering. The Eddas and the Sagas are extraordinary documents, but they are documents, and the practice they describe was already changing as it was being recorded, already filtered through the consciousness of people living in a world that had moved on.

The specific local traditions — the particular gods honored in particular valleys, the specific ritual forms developed by specific communities over specific generations — are almost entirely gone. What we have is a general picture, assembled from sources that represent the whole of Scandinavia and several centuries of change, and the texture of local variation that would have made that general picture so much richer is mostly lost beyond recovery.

The women's traditions, in particular, suffered disproportionately. The völur, the gyðjur, the women who managed the household observances and the álfablót and the dísablót — their practices were the least documented and the most thoroughly suppressed, because they operated in the domestic sphere where the Christian church was both most determined to establish control and least able to observe what was actually happening. We know they existed. We know they were important. We know far less than we should about what they actually did.

These losses matter. Any honest account of what Norse Paganism is today has to reckon with them — has to acknowledge that reconstruction, however careful and however well-sourced, is not the same as continuity, that there are things about the living tradition that we simply do not know and cannot recover.

What Survived

And yet.

The stories survived — assembled, edited, preserved by people who understood their value, passed down through centuries of Christian Scandinavia in manuscripts that were copied and recopied and eventually printed and translated and distributed to readers across the world who had never heard of Snorri Sturluson and could not have told you the difference between the Poetic Edda and the Prose Edda but who found, in the stories themselves, something that spoke to them.

The gods survived — not as objects of worship in any continuous institutional sense, but as figures in the cultural imagination of northern Europe, embedded in the days of the week, the landscapes of the north, the literary traditions that grew from the same soil that produced the Eddas. Tolkien read the Elder Edda as a student and spent the rest of his life working with what he found there. Wagner heard the Ring cycle in the Norse sources and built a monument to them that has been performed continuously for a hundred and fifty years. These are not trivial survivals. They are evidence that the material has a vitality that institutional suppression could not eliminate.

The values survived — embedded in the cultures that developed from Viking Age Scandinavia, expressed in different vocabularies across different centuries, but recognizable in their emphasis on courage, honesty, hospitality, and the dignity of a life lived without illusions about what the world owes you. The specific theological framework fell away. The underlying orientation toward existence did not.

And the practice survived — in modified, diminished, interrupted form, but survived nonetheless — in the household observances that persisted long after the public religion was gone, in the folklore of the Scandinavian countries where the old beings never quite lost their presence in the landscape, in the Sami communities who maintained their own traditions in the far north and who are still there, still practicing, still the oldest living link to the religious world from which Norse Paganism grew.

The Conversation Continues

What has happened in the past century, and especially in the past few decades, is not a resurrection of something dead. It is the emergence of something that was always present, finding the conditions that allowed it to become visible again.

The people who practice Asatru in Iceland today, who have built the Ásatrúarfélagið into the fastest-growing religion in the country, who are constructing the first purpose-built hof on the island since the conversion — they are not recreating the tenth century. They are doing what every generation of religious practitioners does: working with the material they have inherited, in the world as they find it, to build something that makes the experience of being alive more coherent and more meaningful. The fact that the material they are working with is a thousand years old makes the project more demanding, not less genuine.

The scholars who study the Norse sources — the runologists, the archaeologists, the philologists, the historians — are part of the same conversation, approached from a different angle. Every new runestone excavated, every new archaeological site analyzed, every new close reading of the Eddic poems adds to the picture that practitioners and scholars share. The picture will never be complete. It will always be a puzzle with pieces missing, assembled from fragments, requiring inference where certainty is unavailable. This is not a deficiency. It is the nature of working with the past, and the Norse tradition is no more incomplete than any other ancient religion whose sources have survived in partial form.

The conversation between the mythological tradition and the wider culture continues as well. The Marvel Cinematic Universe's Thor is not the Norse Thor — he is something else, a figure made from Norse parts, assembled for different purposes. But he has introduced millions of people to names and stories they would not otherwise have encountered, and some of those people have followed the trail back to the Eddas. The path from a film to a theological text is an unusual one, but it is a path, and it has been walked more often than you might expect.

What the Tradition Asks

Norse Paganism is not a comfortable religion. It has never been one, and the people who practice it in its most faithful forms today seem to understand this and embrace it.

It asks you to take seriously the idea that the world is complex and dangerous and does not owe you a favorable outcome. It asks you to honor powers that are genuinely powerful rather than simply reassuring — gods who struggle, who sacrifice, who make catastrophic mistakes and live with the consequences. It asks you to keep faith with your ancestors and your community in ways that create real obligations rather than merely nominal ones. It asks you to face the fact that everything ends — that the world itself ends — and to find in that fact not despair but the specific motivation to live well while living is possible.

These are hard things. They are also true things, or true enough to be worth orienting a life around. That, in the end, is what any religious tradition worth the name offers: not certainty, not comfort in any simple sense, but a framework within which the actual conditions of human existence become navigable. A way of seeing that makes the difficulty bearable and the beauty visible and the obligations clear.

The Norse tradition does this with particular honesty. Its gods are not perfect. Its cosmos is not designed for human comfort. Its eschatology is not optimistic in any straightforward sense. But within all of that, it offers something genuinely sustaining: the example of beings who faced impossible odds with courage and generosity, who valued what they had because they knew it was temporary, who found meaning not in the guarantee of a good outcome but in the quality of what they did while the outcome was still uncertain.

This is what the Vikings were reaching for when they raised a horn to Odin before a battle. This is what the völva was accessing when she entered her trance and spoke the fates of the people gathered around her. This is what the family performing the álfablót in their closed house understood when they left food out for the spirits of the land and the dead. This is what the modern practitioner is trying to recover when they sit down with the Eddas and ask themselves what it might mean to live by these stories rather than merely to know them.

A Final Word

We began this book ten thousand years ago, in a land that had no name yet, with people who left behind almost nothing except the suggestion of spiritual life. We end it in the present, with a tradition that has survived suppression and centuries of underground existence to emerge, battered but recognizable, into a world that it did not expect and has had to learn to navigate.

The thread that runs between those two points is not unbroken. It has been cut and knotted and stretched and frayed, and anyone who tells you otherwise is selling something. But it is there — in the stories, in the values, in the names of the days of the week, in the archaeological record of every offering buried in the ground and every runestone raised beside a road, in the ongoing practice of communities that have decided these ancient stories still have something to say.

The world tree is still standing. Níðhöggr is still gnawing at its roots. The Norns are still weaving. Odin is still sending his ravens out each morning and waiting for them to return with news of what is happening across the nine worlds.

And somewhere, in Iceland and in America and in Germany and in Australia and in a hundred other places that the Vikings never reached, someone is lifting a horn and saying a name that is more than a thousand years old.

Skol.

Glossary

Aegir — Giant of the deep ocean, husband of Rán. Known for hosting feasts attended by the Aesir gods in his underwater hall.

Aesir — The principal tribe of Norse gods, resident in Asgard. Associated with war, wisdom, and sovereignty. Includes Odin, Thor, Frigg, and Tyr.

Alfheim — The world of the light elves, given to the god Freyr as a gift. Located close to Asgard.

Álfablót — A private household ritual performed in autumn to honor the elves and ancestral spirits. One of the most tenacious survivals after Christianization.

Animism — The belief that all natural objects — animals, plants, rocks, rivers — possess a spirit and a will of their own.

Ansuz — The fourth rune of the Elder Futhark, associated with Odin, divine communication, poetry, and inspired wisdom.

Asatru — The largest modern Norse Pagan path, meaning "true to the Aesir." Formally recognized as a religion in Iceland in 1973.

Askr — The first man in Norse mythology, made from an ash tree by Odin, Vili, and Vé.

Asgard — The highest of the nine worlds, home of the Aesir tribe of gods. Connected to Midgard by the rainbow bridge Bifrost.

Auðumbla — The primordial cow who emerged from the melting ice of Ginnungagap alongside Ymir, sustaining him with her milk.

Berkano — The eighteenth rune of the Elder Futhark, associated with the birch tree, birth, growth, and feminine cycles of renewal.

Bifrost — The rainbow bridge connecting Midgard to Asgard. Guarded by Heimdall and said to burn with fire that only the gods can safely cross.

Blót — The sacrificial feast at the center of Norse ritual practice. An offering of food, drink, or animals made to the gods or other supernatural powers in exchange for continued favor.

Dagaz — The twenty-third rune of the Elder Futhark, associated with the dawn, breakthrough, and transformative thresholds between states.

Dísablót — A late-winter festival honoring the dísir — female ancestral spirits associated with fate and domestic fertility.

Dísir — Female ancestral spirits tied to a specific family line. Associated with fate, protection, and the fertility of the household.

Dökkálfar — The dark elves of Norse mythology, whose distinction from the dwarves remains unclear in the sources.

Draugr — The restless dead — a corporeal undead figure in Norse belief, associated with improper burial or unresolved attachment to life.

Edda — The collective name for the two primary literary sources of Norse mythology: the Poetic Edda, a collection of anonymous poems, and the Prose Edda, written by Snorri Sturluson around 1220.

Ehwaz — The nineteenth rune of the Elder Futhark, associated with the horse, partnership, and trust between two beings working together.

Eihwaz — The thirteenth rune of the Elder Futhark, associated with the yew tree, the axis between worlds, and the coexistence of life and death.

Einherjar — The chosen slain who reside in Valhalla, training daily for the battle of Ragnarök.

Embla — The first woman in Norse mythology, made from an elm tree by Odin, Vili, and Vé.

Ergi — A Norse term for unmanliness, used as a social stigma against men who practiced seiðr magic, which was considered a feminine domain.

Fólkvangr — The Field of the People, Freya's hall where she receives half of all warriors who fall in battle.

Fehu — The first rune of the Elder Futhark, associated with cattle, wealth, and the responsibilities of material prosperity.

Fenrir — The monstrous wolf, son of Loki and the giantess Angrboða. Bound by the gods with a magical ribbon until Ragnarök, when he will break free and swallow Odin.

Futhark — The runic alphabet, named after its first six characters. The Elder Futhark consists of twenty-four runes; the Younger Futhark, used during the Viking Age, was reduced to sixteen.

Galdr — Incantatory magic performed through sung or chanted verses. Used for healing, protection, cursing, and communication with the dead.

Gebo — The seventh rune of the Elder Futhark, associated with the gift and the reciprocal obligations that gift exchange creates.

Ginnungagap — The primordial void that existed before creation — not empty, but charged with latent power, where ice from Niflheim and fire from Muspelheim met to produce the first life.

Gjallarhorn — The great horn held by Heimdall, whose sound will signal the beginning of Ragnarök and summon the gods to their final battle.

Goði — A Norse priest-chieftain responsible for conducting rituals, managing the temple, and representing the community in its relationship with the gods.

Gyðja — The female counterpart of the goði, a ritual leader and religious authority within the Norse community.

Hagalaz — The ninth rune of the Elder Futhark, associated with hail, sudden disruption, and the destructive forces of nature.

Haustblót — The autumn harvest sacrifice, held to give thanks for the year's abundance and to ask for continued protection through the winter.

Heiðrún — The goat who feeds on the leaves of Yggdrasil and produces the endless mead drunk by the einherjar in Valhalla each night.

Heimdall — The watchman of Asgard, stationed at the top of Bifrost. Possesses extraordinary sight and hearing. Holds the Gjallarhorn.

Hel — Both the realm of the ordinary dead and its ruler, daughter of Loki. Not a place of punishment, but of diminished continuation — a permanent twilight for those who did not die in battle.

Hof — A dedicated Norse ritual building, equivalent to a temple, used for seasonal festivals and public sacrifices.

Huginn and Muninn — Odin's two ravens, whose names mean Thought and Memory. They fly across the nine worlds each day and return to report what they have seen.

Ingwaz — The twenty-second rune of the Elder Futhark, associated with the god Freyr, stored potential, and the gestation period between action and result.

Isa — The eleventh rune of the Elder Futhark, associated with ice, stillness, and the suspension of movement or change.

Jera — The twelfth rune of the Elder Futhark, associated with the year, the harvest, and the reward of patient, faithful labor.

Jörmungandr — The Midgard Serpent, child of Loki, cast into the ocean by Odin. Grown large enough to encircle the world and hold its own tail. Thor's destined opponent at Ragnarök.

Jotunheim — The homeland of the giants, surrounding Midgard at the edges of the known world. Rocky, forested, and perpetually frozen.

Kaunan — The sixth rune of the Elder Futhark, associated with the torch, controlled fire, and the pain that burns from within.

Kindred — The local worship community in modern Asatru practice. The basic social unit of contemporary Norse Paganism.

Laguz — The twenty-first rune of the Elder Futhark, associated with water, the sea, and the unconscious forces that cannot be contained.

Loki — A shape-shifting trickster of ambiguous divine status, neither fully Aesir nor giant. Responsible for Baldr's death and ultimately aligned against the gods at Ragnarök.

Ljósálfar — The light elves of Norse mythology, described as fairer than the sun to look upon. Associated with fertility and the benevolent forces of nature.

Mannaz — The twentieth rune of the Elder Futhark, associated with the human being as a social creature — the self embedded in community and obligation.

Midgard — The world of humans, located at the center of the cosmic structure, made from Ymir's flesh by Odin and his brothers.

Mjölnir — Thor's hammer, forged by the dwarves. Capable of destroying any foe, channeling lightning, and consecrating marriages, births, and the dead.

Muspelheim — The primordial world of fire, one of the two realms that existed before creation. Home of the fire giants and their ruler Surtr.

Nauthiz — The tenth rune of the Elder Futhark, associated with need, constraint, and the formative power of endured hardship.

Nidavellir — The underground world of the dwarves, the greatest craftsmen in the nine realms. Also called Svartalfheim in some sources.

Niflheim — The primordial world of mist and ice, one of the two realms that existed before creation. Located beneath the roots of Yggdrasil.

Níðhöggr — The dragon who gnaws perpetually at the roots of Yggdrasil from below, embodying the slow entropy built into the structure of the cosmos.

Noaidi — A Sami shaman, specialist in navigating the boundary between the visible world and the spirit world through trance, drumming, and chanting.

Norns — Three female beings — Urðr, Verðandi, and Skuld — who weave the threads of fate for all living beings at the Well of Urðr beneath Yggdrasil. Their decrees cannot be appealed, even by the gods.

Othala — The twenty-fourth rune of the Elder Futhark, associated with the ancestral estate, inherited identity, and the obligations of belonging to a lineage.

Perthro — The fourteenth rune of the Elder Futhark, associated with fate, chance, and the element of the unknown within the weaving of destiny.

Polytheism — The belief in multiple gods and divine powers, a defining characteristic of both Sami shamanism and Norse Paganism.

Prima Signatio — A preliminary marking with the sign of the cross, adopted by Norse traders to gain access to Christian markets without committing to full baptism.

Raidho — The fifth rune of the Elder Futhark, associated with the journey, ordered movement, and the proper conduct of travel through the world.

Ragnarök — The prophesied destruction of the cosmos — a final battle between the gods and the forces of chaos in which most divine beings perish and the world is consumed. Followed, in the Christianized version of the myth, by renewal.

Rán — Giantess of the sea, wife of Ægir. Said to drag drowning travelers to her underwater hall with a net.

Ratatoskr — The squirrel who runs up and down the trunk of Yggdrasil carrying insults between the eagle in the branches and the dragon Níðhöggr at the roots.

Rökkr — The dark gods of Norse mythology — Hel, Loki, Fenrir, Jörmungandr, and others — who represent chaos, destruction, and the forces that oppose the Aesir. The focus of the Rökkatru path.

Rökkatru — A modern Norse Pagan path oriented toward the Rökkr, the dark deities of Norse mythology. Understands chaos and destruction as necessary cosmic forces rather than simple evil.

Saivo — The Sami concept of the afterlife — not a place of judgment but an abundant mirror of the physical world, where the dead continued their existence in improved conditions.

Seiðr — A form of high ritual magic practiced primarily by women, used to perceive and alter the threads of fate. Associated with the goddess Freya, who taught it to Odin.

Sigrblót — A spring festival marking the beginning of summer and blessing the season's raiding, trading, and agricultural ventures. Primarily associated with Odin.

Skáldskaparmál — The third section of Snorri Sturluson's Prose Edda, consisting of extensive lists of poetic kennings and heiti used in skaldic verse.

Sleipnir — Odin's eight-legged horse, the fastest in the nine worlds. Born from Loki in mare form during the construction of Asgard's wall.

Sowilo — The sixteenth rune of the Elder Futhark, associated with the sun, victory, and the force that drives away darkness.

Sturluson, Snorri — Icelandic poet, politician, and scholar (1179–1241), author of the Prose Edda. The single most important source for Norse mythology as a coherent system.

Sumbel — A ritualized drinking ceremony in which participants make toasts to the gods, the ancestors, and personal vows. Speeches made during a sumbel carry binding social weight.

Surtr — The ruler of Muspelheim, a fire giant armed with a flaming sword. Destined to lead the forces of destruction at Ragnarök and burn the world to nothing.

Thurisaz — The third rune of the Elder Futhark, associated with giants, directed force, and the double-edged nature of overwhelming power.

Tiwaz — The seventeenth rune of the Elder Futhark, associated with the god Tyr, justice, and the willingness to sacrifice personally for the greater good.

Thrall — An enslaved person in Viking Age Scandinavia, acquired primarily through raids and used for the most physically demanding agricultural and domestic labor.

Thing — The Norse legal assembly where disputes were resolved, laws recited, and community decisions made. A foundational institution of Norse social organization.

Uruz — The second rune of the Elder Futhark, associated with the wild aurochs, untamed vitality, and the raw strength of the natural world before domestication.

Valhalla — The Hall of the Slain in Asgard, where Odin receives warriors chosen by the Valkyries. The einherjar who dwell there train daily for the battle of Ragnarök.

Valkyries — Odin's female agents who move through battlefields determining which warriors fall and carrying the chosen dead to Valhalla. Their name means "choosers of the slain."

Vanatru — A modern Norse Pagan path centered on the Vanir gods — Freya, Freyr, and Njord — with an emphasis on nature, fertility, magic, and individual spiritual experience.

Vanaheim — The world of the Vanir tribe of gods, associated with fertility and nature. The least described of the nine worlds in the surviving sources.

Vanir — The second tribe of Norse gods, associated with fertility, nature, and magic. Includes Freya, Freyr, and Njord. Fought a war with the Aesir that ended in a permanent exchange of hostages.

Varðlokur — Songs used during seiðr rituals to call the spirits that would assist the völva in her trance journey through the spirit world.

Vé — One of Odin's two brothers, alongside Vili. Together the three brothers killed Ymir and built the world from his body.

Völuspá — "The Insight of the Seeress," one of the most important poems in the Poetic Edda. Narrated by a völva summoned by Odin, it describes the creation of the world and its destruction at Ragnarök.

Völva — A Norse seeress and professional practitioner of seiðr magic. A traveling specialist who moved between communities, performing divination and fate-working for payment.

Wunjo — The eighth rune of the Elder Futhark, associated with joy, harmony, and the pleasure of a community functioning as it should.

Wyrd — The Old Norse and Old English concept of fate or destiny — the web of consequences woven by the Norns that connects all beings and all events.

Yggdrasil — The World Tree, an immense ash at the center of the Norse cosmos whose branches hold the nine worlds and whose roots extend into Asgard, Jotunheim, and Niflheim.

Ymir — The first being, who condensed from the meeting of ice and fire in Ginnungagap. Killed by Odin, Vili, and Vé, whose body was used to build the world.

Yule — The Norse midwinter festival lasting twelve days, centered on the winter solstice. Associated with Odin, ancestor veneration, feasting, and the return of the sun. The most enduring of all Norse festivals in the modern world.

References

Primary Sources

Larrington, Carolyne, trans. *The Poetic Edda*. Oxford University Press, 2014.

Sturluson, Snorri. *The Prose Edda*. Translated by Jesse Byock. Penguin Classics, 2005.

Sturluson, Snorri. *Heimskringla: History of the Kings of Norway*. Translated by Lee M. Hollander. University of Texas Press, 1964.

The Völsunga Saga. Translated by Jesse Byock. Penguin Classics, 1999.

Egil's Saga. Translated by Bernard Scudder. Penguin Classics, 2004.

Ibn Fadlan, Ahmad. *Ibn Fadlan and the Land of Darkness: Arab Travellers in the Far North*. Translated by Paul Lunde and Caroline Stone. Penguin Classics, 2012.

History and Archaeology

Winroth, Anders. *The Age of the Vikings*. Princeton University Press, 2016.

Roesdahl, Else. *The Vikings*. Revised edition. Penguin Books, 2016.

Graham-Campbell, James. *The Viking World*. Frances Lincoln, 2013.

Price, Neil. *The Children of Ash and Elm: A History of the Vikings*. Basic Books, 2020.

Gundersen, Margit Petersen. "Scandinavia Before the Vikings." *Life in Norway*, 2020.

Adam of Bremen. *History of the Archbishops of Hamburg-Bremen*. Translated by Francis J. Tschan. Columbia University Press, 2002.

Mythology and Religion

Price, Neil S. *The Viking Way: Religion and War in Late Iron Age Scandinavia*. Oxbow Books, 2019.

McCoy, Daniel. *Norse Mythology for Smart People*. norse-mythology.org, 2012.

Simek, Rudolf. *Dictionary of Northern Mythology*. D.S. Brewer, 2007.

Lindow, John. *Norse Mythology: A Guide to Gods, Heroes, Rituals, and Beliefs*. Oxford University Press, 2001.

Orchard, Andy. *Dictionary of Norse Myth and Legend*. Cassell, 1997.

Holloway, April. "The Decline of the Sami People's Indigenous Religion." *Ancient Origins*, n.d.

Magic, Runes, and Ritual

Page, R.I. *Runes*. British Museum Press, 1987.

Ongkowidjojo, Vincent. "On the Origins of the Runes: Symbols, Mysteries and Magico-Religious Concepts." 2016.

Aswynn, Freya. *Northern Mysteries and Magick: Runes and Feminine Powers*. Llewellyn Publications, 1998.

Paxson, Diana L. *Taking Up the Runes: A Complete Guide to Using Runes in Spells, Rituals, Divination, and Magic*. Weiser Books, 2005.

Viking Archaeology. "Seidr." viking.archeurope.info, n.d.

Bronze Age and Iron Age

Editors of Encyclopedia Britannica. "Bronze Age." *Encyclopædia Britannica*, 2021.

Burrows, Hannah A. *The Poetic Edda: Völuspá*. 1936. Revised edition, 2019.

"Bronze Age Scandinavia." encyclopedia.com, n.d.

"Everyday Life in Viking Times." *Q-Files Encyclopedia: History, Vikings*, 2022.

Christianization and Conversion

"Christianity Comes to Denmark." National Museum of Denmark, 2019.

Hrafnhild, N., and Svartsesol. *An Introduction to Vanatru*. Lulu Enterprises, 2010.

Story, Joanna. "The Viking Raid on Lindisfarne." English Heritage, 2019.

Adams, Simon. "Lindisfarne Raid." *Encyclopædia Britannica*, 2018.

Modern Practice

Wigington, Patti. "What Is the Asatru Pagan Tradition?" *Learn Religions*, 2019.

Greenberg, Mike, PhD. "The Aesir-Vanir War." *Mythology Source*, 2020.

Hurstwic Norse Mythology. "The First War." hurstwic.org, n.d.

Blot. *The Asatru Community*, n.d.

Rituals. Gudavik, n.d.

Nomads, Time. "Norse Paganism for Beginners: Quick Introduction and Resources." *Time Nomads*, 2021.

Further Reading

Byock, Jesse. *Viking Age Iceland*. Penguin Books, 2001.

Clunies Ross, Margaret. *A History of Old Norse Poetry and Poetics*. D.S. Brewer, 2005.

DuBois, Thomas A. *Nordic Religions in the Viking Age*. University of Pennsylvania Press, 1999.

Hedeager, Lotte. *Iron Age Myth and Materiality: An Archaeology of Scandinavia AD 400–1000*. Routledge, 2011.

Jesch, Judith. *Women in the Viking Age*. Boydell Press, 1991.

Jochens, Jenny. *Old Norse Images of Women*. University of Pennsylvania Press, 1996.

A Note to the Reader

If this book has been useful to you — if it has given you a clearer sense of who the Norse people were, what they believed, and why those beliefs still matter — I would be genuinely grateful if you took a few minutes to leave a review on Amazon.

Reviews make an enormous difference for independent authors. They help other readers find the book, and they help me understand what is resonating and what could be better. A sentence or two about what you found valuable is more than enough. Your words carry more weight than you might expect.

Thank you for making this journey with me — from the Sami shamans of the Stone Age to the kindreds practicing today, from the first runestones to Ragnarök. I hope it has left you with a genuine curiosity about this tradition, and perhaps with a few of the gods looking a little more real than they did before.

Skol.

Erik Hansen

www.ingramcontent.com/pod-product-compliance
Lightning Source LLC
Chambersburg PA
CBHW071756120626
46550CB00002B/814

* 9 7 8 1 9 6 1 9 6 3 5 5 9 *